STRENGTHSFINDER 2.0
FROM GALLUP
and *Tom Rath*

Discover Your
CliftonStrengths

GALLUP PRESS
1330 Avenue of the Americas
17th Floor
New York, NY 10019

Library of Congress Control Number: 2006938575
ISBN: 978-1-59562-015-6

First Printing: 2007
43

CliftonStrengths version 2017

Copyright © 2007 Gallup, Inc.
All rights reserved, including the right of reproduction in whole or in part in any form.

Gallup®, CliftonStrengths®, Clifton StrengthsFinder®, Gallup Press®, Q12®, StrengthsFinder® and the 34 CliftonStrengths theme names are trademarks of Gallup, Inc. All other trademarks are property of their respective owners.

The Q^{12} items are Gallup proprietary information and are protected by law. You may not administer a survey with the Q^{12} items or reproduce them without written consent from Gallup. Copyright © 1993-1998 Gallup, Inc. All rights reserved.

Printed in Canada

♻ This book was printed on chlorine-free paper made with 100% post-consumer waste.

NOTE TO READERS

In 2017, Gallup changed the name of the StrengthsFinder assessment to CliftonStrengths in honor of Don Clifton, inventor of the assessment and Father of Strengths-Based Psychology.

Don Clifton
(1924-2003)

Inventor of CliftonStrengths® and recognized as the
Father of Strengths-Based Psychology by an American
Psychological Association Presidential Commendation

CONTENTS

CliftonStrengths: The Next Generation.................... I

**PART I: Finding Your Strengths —
             An Introduction** 1

PART II: Applying Your Strengths......................33

The 34 Themes and Ideas for Action
    Achiever..37
    Activator 41
    Adaptability 45
    Analytical 49
    Arranger..53
    Belief..57
    Command...61
    Communication 65
    Competition...69
    Connectedness 73
    Consistency..77
    Context 81
    Deliberative..85
    Developer...89

Discipline	93
Empathy	97
Focus	101
Futuristic	105
Harmony	109
Ideation	113
Includer	117
Individualization	121
Input	125
Intellection	129
Learner	133
Maximizer	137
Positivity	141
Relator	145
Responsibility	149
Restorative	153
Self-Assurance	157
Significance	161
Strategic	165
Woo	169

VFAQ (VERY Frequently Asked Question) 173

CLIFTONSTRENGTHS:
THE NEXT GENERATION

In 1998, I began working with a team of Gallup scientists led by the late Father of Strengths-Based Psychology, Don Clifton. Our goal was to start a global conversation about what's right with people.

We were tired of living in a world that revolved around fixing our weaknesses. Society's relentless focus on people's shortcomings had turned into a global obsession. What's more, we had discovered that people have several times more potential for growth when they invest energy in developing their strengths instead of correcting their deficiencies.

Based on Gallup's 40-year study of human strengths, we created a language of the 34 most common talents and developed the original CliftonStrengths assessment to help people discover and describe these talents. Then in 2001, we included the initial version of this assessment with the bestselling management book *Now, Discover Your Strengths*. The discussion quickly moved beyond the management audience of that book. It appears that the world was ready to have this conversation.

Over the past few years, millions of people have taken the CliftonStrengths assessment and learned about their top five themes of talent — and *Now, Discover Your Strengths* spent more than five years on the bestseller lists. The assessment has since been translated into more than 20 languages and is used by businesses, schools and community groups in more than 100 nations around the world. Yet when it comes to creating strengths-based families, communities and workplaces, we still have a lot of work to do.

Over the past decade, Gallup has surveyed more than 10 million people worldwide on the topic of employee engagement (or how positive and productive people are at work), and only one-third "strongly agree" with the statement:

"At work, I have the opportunity to do what I do best every day."

And for those who do *not* get to focus on what they do best — their strengths — the costs are staggering. In a recent poll of more than 1,000 people, among those who "strongly disagreed" or "disagreed" with this "what I do best" statement, *not one single person* was emotionally engaged on the job.

In stark contrast, our studies indicate that people who *do* have the opportunity to focus on their strengths every day are *six times as likely to be engaged in their jobs* and more than *three times as likely to report having an excellent quality of life in general*.

Fortunately, our research also suggests that having someone at work who regularly focuses on your strengths can make a dramatic difference. In 2005, we explored what happens when managers primarily focus on employees' strengths, primarily focus on employees' weaknesses or ignore employees. What we found completely redefined my perspective about how easy it may be to decrease the active disengagement, or extreme negativity, that runs rampant in organizations.

If your manager primarily:	The chances of your being actively disengaged are:
Ignores you	*40%*
Focuses on your weaknesses	*22%*
Focuses on your strengths	*1%*

As you can see from these results, having a manager who ignores you is even more detrimental than having a manager who primarily focuses on your weaknesses. Perhaps most surprising is the degree to which having a manager who focuses on your strengths decreases the odds of your being miserable on the job. It appears that the epidemic of active disengagement we see in workplaces every day could be a curable disease ... if we can help the people around us develop their strengths.

What's New in CliftonStrengths?

Our research and knowledge base on the topic of human strengths have expanded dramatically over the past decade. The CliftonStrengths assessment included with this book picks up where the original version left off, and it is designed to provide you with the latest discoveries and strategies for application. The language of 34 themes remains the same, but the assessment is faster and even more reliable. And, the results yield a much more in-depth analysis of your strengths.

Once you have completed the online assessment, you will have access to personalized reports and tools, including a comprehensive strengths development guide that is based on your CliftonStrengths results. This guide features an in-depth dive into the nuances of what makes you unique, using more than 5,000 personalized Strengths Insights that we have discovered in recent years.

Going far beyond the shared theme descriptions, which can be found in Part II of this book, these highly customized Strengths Insights will help you understand how each of your top five themes plays out in your life on a much more personal level. For example, even though you and a friend may both have the same theme in your top five, the way this theme is manifested will not be the same. Therefore, each of you would receive entirely different, personalized descriptions of how that theme operates in your lives. These Strengths Insights describe *what makes you stand out* when compared with the millions of people we have studied.

The guide also includes 10 "Ideas for Action" for each of your top five themes. So, you will have 50 specific actions you can take — ideas we culled from thousands of best-practice suggestions — that are customized to your top five themes. In addition, the guide will help you build a strengths-based development plan by exploring how your greatest natural talents interact with your skills, knowledge and experience. And the website includes several other resources you can use to learn more about your strengths and the strengths of others.

While learning about your strengths may be an interesting experience, it offers little benefit in isolation. This book, assessment, website and development guide are all about application. If you want to improve your life and the lives of those around you, you must take action. Use the personalized development guide to align your job and goals with your natural talents. Share this plan with your coworkers, boss or closest friends. Then help the people around you — at work and at home — develop their strengths. If you do, chances are you will find yourself in a much more positive and productive environment.

PART I:
FINDING YOUR STRENGTHS — AN INTRODUCTION

THE PATH OF *MOST* RESISTANCE

At its fundamentally flawed core, the aim of almost any learning program is to help us become who we are *not*. If you don't have natural talent with numbers, you're still forced to spend time in that area to attain a degree. If you're not very empathic, you get sent to a course designed to infuse empathy into your personality. From the cradle to the cubicle, we devote more time to our shortcomings than to our strengths.

This is quite apparent in the way we create icons out of people who struggle to overcome a lack of natural talent. Consider the true story of Rudy Ruettiger, the 23-year-old groundskeeper at Notre Dame's stadium, who was the protagonist of the 1993 movie *Rudy*. At just 5'6" and 165 pounds, this young man clearly didn't possess the physical ability to play big-time college football, but he had ample "heart."

Rudy worked tirelessly to gain admission to Notre Dame so he could play football there. Eventually, after being rejected three times, he was accepted at Notre Dame and soon thereafter earned a spot on the football team's practice squad.

For two years, Rudy took a beating in daily practices, but he was never allowed to join his team on the sidelines. Then, after trying as hard as he could for two seasons, Rudy was finally invited to suit up for the final game of his senior year. In the last moments of this game, with a Notre Dame victory safely in hand, Rudy's teammates lobbied their coach to put him in the game. In the final seconds, the coach sent Rudy in for a single play — and he tackled the opposing team's quarterback.

It was a dramatic moment and, of course, Rudy became an instant hero. Fans chanted his name and carried him off the field. Ruettiger was later invited to the White House, where he met President Bill Clinton, Colin Powell and football legend Joe Montana. While Rudy's perseverance is admirable, in the end, he played a few seconds of college football and made a single tackle ... after thousands of hours of practicing.

The inspirational nature of this story actually masks a significant problem: Overcoming deficits is an essential part of the fabric of our culture. Our books, movies and folklore are filled with stories of the underdog who beats one-in-a-million odds. And this leads us to celebrate those who triumph over their lack of natural ability even more than we recognize those who capitalize on their innate talents. As a result, millions of people see these heroes as being the epitome of the American Dream and set their sights on conquering major challenges. Unfortunately, this is taking the path of *most* resistance.

A Misguided Maxim?

"You can be anything you want to be, if you just try hard enough."

Like most people, I embraced this maxim at a young age. Along with thousands of other kids, I spent a good chunk of my childhood trying to be the next Michael Jordan. Every day, I practiced shooting hoops for three to four hours. I went to basketball camps each summer and tried in every way possible to be a great player. No matter how hard I worked at it, though, becoming an NBA star simply wasn't in the cards for me. After giving 100% of my effort for more than five years, I couldn't even make the *junior* varsity team.

Embracing the "You-can-be-anything-you-want-to-be" maxim isn't something we outgrow. Similar scenarios play out in the workplace every day. Star salespeople think they can be great sales managers with enough effort. They interview other managers to gain insight, read every book on management they can find and stay late every night trying to get the job done — at the expense of their family and even their health. Then, a few years into the job, they realize that they don't have the natural talent to develop other people. Not only is this a waste of their time, but chances are, they could have increased their contribution even more if they had stayed in the sales role — a role in which they naturally excelled. Yet if we want additional income, status or responsibility, most organizational hierarchies force us into a very different role — instead of allowing for an entire career of progression within a specific role that fits our talents.

What's even more disheartening is the way our fixation on deficits affects young people in the home and classroom. In every culture we have studied, the overwhelming majority of parents (77% in the United States) think that a student's *lowest* grades deserve the *most* time and attention. Parents and teachers reward excellence with apathy instead of investing more time in the areas where a child has the most potential for greatness.

The reality is that a person who has always struggled with numbers is unlikely to be a great accountant or statistician. And the person without much natural empathy will never be able to comfort an agitated customer in the warm and sincere way that the great empathizers can. Even the legendary Michael Jordan, who embodied the power of raw talent on a basketball court, could not become, well, the "Michael Jordan" of golf or baseball, no matter how hard he tried.

This might sound like a heretical point of view, especially for those of us who grew up believing the essential American myth that we could become anything we wanted. Yet it's clear from Gallup's research that each person has greater potential for success in specific areas, and the key to human development is building on who you *already are*.

The following real-life example from Gallup's economic development work in Puebla, Mexico, provides a basic yet powerful illustration of what can happen when people focus on their natural talents.

Hector had always been known as a great shoemaker. In fact, customers from such far-off places as France claimed that Hector made the best shoes in the world. Yet for years, he had been frustrated with his small shoemaking business. Although Hector knew he was capable of making hundreds of shoes per week, he was averaging just 30 pairs. When a friend asked him why, Hector explained that while he was great at producing shoes, he was a poor salesman — and terrible when it came to collecting payments. Yet he spent most of his time working in these areas of weakness.

So, Hector's friend introduced him to Sergio, a natural salesman and marketer. Just as Hector was known for his craftsmanship, Sergio could close deals and sell. Given the way their strengths complemented one another, Hector and Sergio decided to work together. A year later, this strengths-based duo was producing, selling and collecting payment for more than 100 pairs of shoes per week — a more than threefold increase.

While this story may seem simplistic, in many cases, aligning yourself with the right task can be this easy. When we're able to put most of our energy into developing our natural talents, extraordinary room for growth exists. So, a revision to the "You-can-be-anything-you-want-to-be" maxim might be more accurate:

*You **cannot** be anything you want to be — but you **can** be a lot more of who you already are.*

THE STRENGTHS ZONE

Over the past few decades, Gallup has studied how talent can be applied in a wide variety of roles, from housekeepers to chief executives and from clergy members to government officials. We've researched almost every major culture, country, industry and position. The good news is that we have found great examples of heroes who are soaring with their strengths in every single role. Across the board, having the opportunity to develop our strengths is more important to our success than our role, our title or even our pay. In this increasingly talent-driven society, we need to know and develop our strengths to figure out where we fit in.

That being said, across all areas we have studied, the vast majority of people don't have the opportunity to focus on what they do best. We have surveyed more than 10 million people on this specific topic, and *approximately 7 million are falling short.*

What happens when you're not in the "strengths zone"? You're quite simply a very different person. In the workplace, you are *six times* less likely to be engaged in your job. When you're not able to use your strengths at work, chances are that you:

- dread going to work
- have more negative than positive interactions with your colleagues
- treat your customers poorly
- tell your friends what a miserable company you work for
- achieve less on a daily basis
- have fewer positive and creative moments

Beyond the world of work, there are even more serious implications for your health and relationships if you're not in the strengths zone. And Gallup's research has shown how a strengths-based approach improves your confidence, direction, hope and kindness toward others.

So why isn't everyone living life with a strengths approach? One big problem is that most people are either unaware of, or unable to describe, their own strengths ... or the strengths of the people around them.

YOUR THEMES OF TALENT

"Most people think they know what they are good at. They are usually wrong. ... And yet, a person can perform only from strength."

— Business guru Peter Drucker (1909-2005)

In the mid-1960s, my late mentor and the Father of Strengths-Based Psychology, Don Clifton, realized that we already had countless "languages" for describing what's wrong with people. In addition to the informal labels used by the people around us, the field of psychology has the DSM-IV, a manual of disorders described by one leading psychologist as "a bloated catalogue of what's wrong with people." The world of business has myriad competency models, most of which are oriented toward describing what isn't working (even though these labels are often veiled as "areas for improvement").

To initiate more conversation about what's *right* with people, in 1998, Clifton assembled a team of scientists and set forth the ambitious goal of developing a common language for talent. This team wanted individuals and organizations to have very specific terms for describing what people do well. So we mined our database, which at the time contained more than 100,000 talent-based interviews, and looked for patterns in the data. We examined specific questions that had been used in our studies of successful executives, salespeople, customer service representatives, teachers, doctors, lawyers, students, nurses, and several other professions and fields. Through this process, we were able to identify 34 themes of talent that were the most common in our database. We then developed the first version of the CliftonStrengths assessment to measure these distinct talents.

These 34 themes represent our best attempt at creating a common language or classification of talents. By no means did we capture everything. There are hundreds of even more specific themes we did not include in this classification. However, we wanted to keep this language manageable so it would be easy to use with work teams, families and friends.

What the CliftonStrengths assessment actually measures is talent, not strength. But the ultimate goal is to build a true strength, and talent is just one of the ingredients in this formula. The assessment doesn't ask about your knowledge — there are no questions about your formal education, degrees or résumé. Nor does it ask about your skills — whether you're able to perform the fundamental steps of driving a car, using a particular software package or selling a specific product. While these are important, we have discovered that knowledge and skills — along with regular practice — are most helpful when they serve as amplifiers for your natural talents.

When you take the assessment, you have just 20 seconds to respond to each item. It's quick because we found that instinctual, top-of-mind responses are more revealing than those you'd give if you sat around and debated each question. Essentially, the instrument is attempting to identify your most intense natural responses, which are less likely to change over time.

A Recipe for Strength

Although people certainly *do* change over time and our personalities adapt, scientists have discovered that core personality traits are relatively stable throughout adulthood, as are our passions and interests. And more recent research suggests that the roots of our personality might be visible at an even younger age than was originally thought. A compelling 23-year longitudinal study of 1,000 children in New Zealand revealed that a child's observed personality at age 3 shows remarkable similarity to their reported personality traits at age 26.[*] This is one of the reasons why the CliftonStrengths assessment measures the elements of your personality that are less likely to change — your talents.

---

[*] Caspi, A., Harrington, H., Milne, B., Amell, J.W., Theodore, R.F., & Moffitt, T.E. (2003). Children's behavioral styles at age 3 are linked to their adult personality traits at age 26. *Journal of Personality, 71*, 495-514.

Knowledge, skills and practice are also important parts of the strengths equation. Without basic facts in your mind and skills at your disposal, talent can go untapped. Fortunately, it's also easier to add knowledge and skills to your repertoire. You can always take a course on understanding basic financials, just as you can always learn how to use a new software application. Building your talents into real strengths also requires practice and hard work, much like it does to build physical strengths. For example, if you are born with the potential to build large biceps, but you do not exercise these muscles regularly, they will not develop. However, if you *do* work equally as hard as someone without as much natural potential, you are likely to see much greater return.

But adding raw talent is a very different story. While it may be possible, with a considerable amount of work, to add talent where little exists, our research suggests that this may not be the best use of your time. Instead, we've discovered that the most successful people start with dominant talent — and then add skills, knowledge and practice to the mix. When they do this, the raw talent actually serves as a *multiplier*.

Talent (a natural way of thinking, feeling or behaving)

Investment (time spent practicing, developing your skills and building your knowledge base)

Strength (the ability to consistently provide near-perfect performance)

This brings us back to Rudy Ruettiger, a classic example of hard work offsetting a lack of natural talent to reach a basic level of competence. While Rudy might have scored a perfect 5 on a 1-5 scale for investment (the time he spent practicing and building his knowledge and skills), let's assume he was a 2 on the talent scale. So his maximum potential for building strength in this area was only 10 (5 x 2), even when he scored as high as possible on the investment scale. And it is likely that Rudy had teammates for whom the inverse was true — they were a 5 on talent and just a 2 on time invested, which is clearly a waste of talent. And once in a while, you see a player like former Notre Dame great Joe Montana, who had abundant natural talent combined with hard work and the right developmental opportunities. This combination of a 5 in both areas — which yields a total score of 25, compared with Rudy's score of 10 — is what can elevate someone to an entirely different level.

Even though we recognize that everyone is different, all too often, we give only surface attention to this crucial insight. It is relatively easy to describe our acquired expertise, but most of us struggle when asked to describe our natural talents. If you find it difficult to name all of your talents, take a step back, and you'll see that talents often have something in common — a theme — that connects them. Some talents — like natural tendencies to share thoughts, to create engaging stories and to find the perfect word — are directly connected to communication. That's what they have in common — their theme. So to begin thinking and talking about them, we can call them Communication talents. Other talents — such as natural dependability, sense of commitment and avoidance of excuses — have a responsibility theme, so we identify them as Responsibility talents. This theme language gives us a starting place for discovering our talents and learning even more about our potential for strength.

Managing Weaknesses

In any occupation or role, it's helpful to know your areas of lesser talent. That's especially true if the demands of your job pull you in that direction, as your lesser talents can lead to weakness. As you study the descriptions of the 34 themes, see if you can identify a few areas in which you are clearly lacking in talent and have little potential to create a strength. In many cases, simply being aware of your areas of lesser talent can help you avoid major roadblocks.

Once you're able to acknowledge, for example, that you are not great at managing details, it opens several doors for working around that lesser talent. The first question to ask yourself is whether it's necessary for you to operate in your area of lesser talent at all. If it's possible for you to simply avoid doing detail-oriented work, by all means, move away from this area. Of course, most of us don't have the luxury to simply stop doing necessary tasks just because we aren't naturally good at them. When you must attend to details, you might need to establish systems to manage your lesser talent and keep things on track. If maintaining your daily schedule is a detail you dread, there are several options, ranging from a day planner to an electronic calendar.

Another strategy is to partner with someone who has more talent in the areas in which you are lacking. For example, the Includer theme is an area of lesser talent for me. People who have this talent are great at making sure that everyone feels involved and part of any team effort. On the contrary, I will rush to assemble a group without considering everyone involved, and in many cases, this results in people feeling left out. So I have learned to partner with my colleague Amanda who leads with her Includer. She helps me think about including people I would not have otherwise considered. In several cases, this has helped us uncover people's hidden talents and build a stronger team.

Blind Spots

It is also essential to try to become more conscious of any "blind spots" that are caused by your talents. For example, those of us with strong Command may not realize the damage left in our wake as we are pushing to get things done each day. Or people with dominant Consistency talents might focus so much on keeping the steps uniform that they ignore the overall outcome or goal.

So while our talents primarily serve to keep us on track, they can at times derail our pursuits. In Part II, you will find 10 Ideas for Action for each of the 34 themes. Many of these action items will help you when you are on the lookout for blind spots that can result from your dominant talents. The key is for you to be aware of your potential *and* your limitations.

The Assessment, Website and Development Guide

Analyzing millions of CliftonStrengths interviews has allowed us to refine the assessment into an even faster and more precise version. We've also been working to glean more advanced insights from the hundreds of items we collect as you take the assessment.

Even though the 34 themes help us describe a great deal of the variation in human talent, they do not capture many nuances of unique personalities. While you and a few friends may each have Learner among your top five themes, the fine points of those talents and how they are expressed vary a great deal from person to person: One of you may learn from reading several books each month, while someone else learns primarily from doing, and yet another learns from an insatiable curiosity and Googles everything.

To help you think about your own talents at a more specific and individualized level, we have added more than 5,000 Strengths Insights. Based on unique combinations of your individual item responses during the assessment, these insights will give you an in-depth analysis of how each of your top five themes plays out in your life. Unlike the shared theme descriptions from the original assessment, which are the same for everyone, the descriptions in your updated CliftonStrengths report are customized to describe *your* personality.

To create these highly tailored theme descriptions, we compare all of your responses on these 5,000-plus Strengths Insights to our massive database and then build your theme descriptions based on *what makes you stand out the most*. Unlike your top five themes of talent, which are likely to overlap with people you know and serve an important purpose in providing a common language, the Strengths Insights are all about what makes you unique.

Once you have completed the CliftonStrengths assessment and receive your results, you will have access to reports, tools and resources you can use to learn more about your strengths. And you will get a comprehensive strengths development guide that includes:

- Your top five theme report, built around the updated Strengths Insight descriptions
- 50 Ideas for Action (10 for each of your top five themes) based on thousands of best-practice suggestions we reviewed
- Questions for you to answer to increase your awareness of your talents and how to apply them

PARTING THOUGHTS

Our natural talents and passions — the things we truly love to do — last for a lifetime. But all too often, our talents go untapped. Mark Twain once described a man who died and met Saint Peter at the Pearly Gates. Knowing that Saint Peter was very wise, the man asked a question that he had wondered about throughout his life.

He said, "Saint Peter, I have been interested in military history for many years. Who was the greatest general of all time?"

Saint Peter quickly responded, "Oh that's a simple question. It's that man right over there."

"You must be mistaken," responded the man, now very perplexed. "I knew that man on earth, and he was just a common laborer."

"That's right my friend," assured Saint Peter. "He would have been the greatest general of all time, *if he had been a general*."

This story illustrates a truth that is, unfortunately, all too common. Far too many people spend a lifetime headed in the wrong direction. They go not only from the cradle to the cubicle, but then to the casket, without uncovering their greatest talents and potential.

This is why it's essential not only to discover and develop your strengths as early as possible, but also to help the people around you build on their natural talents. Whether you're helping a good friend realize that they naturally come up with new ideas, supporting a colleague as they look for a better fit for their talents at work, or helping a young person understand that their natural competitiveness could be a lifelong asset instead of a hindrance — these actions will start to change the world around you. Every human being has talents that are just waiting to be uncovered.

TAKING THE CLIFTONSTRENGTHS ASSESSMENT

To help you build on your talents and the talents of the people around you, take the CliftonStrengths assessment now. You will need the unique access code in the packet in the back of this book to take the assessment. It will take about 30 minutes.

After you have completed the assessment, read Part II: Applying Your Strengths. For each of the 34 themes, this section presents the standard theme description, examples of what the theme sounds like, Ideas for Action and tips on how to work with others who have strong talents in that theme.

Remember that the purpose of CliftonStrengths is not to anoint you with strengths — it simply helps you find the areas *where you have the greatest potential to develop strengths.*

PART II:
APPLYING YOUR STRENGTHS

THE 34 THEMES AND IDEAS FOR ACTION

- Achiever
- Activator
- Adaptability
- Analytical
- Arranger
- Belief
- Command
- Communication
- Competition
- Connectedness
- Consistency
- Context
- Deliberative
- Developer
- Discipline
- Empathy
- Focus
- Futuristic
- Harmony
- Ideation
- Includer
- Individualization
- Input
- Intellection
- Learner
- Maximizer
- Positivity
- Relator
- Responsibility
- Restorative
- Self-Assurance
- Significance
- Strategic
- Woo

ACHIEVER

Your Achiever theme helps explain your drive. Achiever describes a constant need for achievement. You feel as if every day starts at zero. By the end of the day you must achieve something tangible in order to feel good about yourself. And by "every day" you mean every single day — workdays, weekends, vacations. No matter how much you may feel you deserve a day of rest, if the day passes without some form of achievement, no matter how small, you will feel dissatisfied. You have an internal fire burning inside you. It pushes you to do more, to achieve more. After each accomplishment is reached, the fire dwindles for a moment, but very soon it rekindles itself, forcing you toward the next accomplishment. Your relentless need for achievement might not be logical. It might not even be focused. But it will always be with you. As an Achiever you must learn to live with this whisper of discontent. It does have its benefits. It brings you the energy you need to work long hours without burning out. It is the jolt you can always count on to get you started on new tasks, new challenges. It is the power supply that causes you to set the pace and define the levels of productivity for your work group. It is the theme that keeps you moving.

Achiever Sounds Like This:

Melanie K., ER nurse: "I have to rack up points every day to feel successful. Today I've been here only half an hour, but I've probably racked up thirty points already. I ordered equipment for the ER, I had equipment repaired, I had a meeting with my charge nurse and I brainstormed with my secretary about improving our computerized logbook. So on my list of ninety things, I have thirty done already. I'm feeling pretty good about myself right now."

Ted S., salesperson: "Last year I was salesperson of the year out of my company's three hundred salespeople. It felt good for a day, but sure enough, later that week, it was as if it never happened. I was back at zero again. Sometimes I wish I wasn't an achiever because it can lead me away from a balanced life and toward obsession. I used to think I could change myself, but now I know I am just wired this way. This theme is truly a double-edged sword. It helps me achieve my goals, but on the other hand, I wish I could just turn it off and on at will. But, hey, I can't. I *can* manage it and avoid work obsession by focusing on achieving in all parts of my life, not just work."

Sara L., writer: "This theme is a weird one. First, it's good because you live in pursuit of the perpetual challenge. But in the second place, you never feel as though you've reached your goal. It can keep you running uphill at seventy miles an hour for your whole life. You never rest because there's always more to do. But, on balance, I think I would rather have it than not. I call it my 'divine restlessness,' and if it makes me feel as if I owe the present everything I have, then so be it. I can live with that."

Ideas for Action

- Select jobs that allow you to have the leeway to work as hard as you want and in which you are encouraged to measure your own productivity. You will feel challenged and alive in these environments.

- As an achiever, you relish the feeling of being busy, yet you also need to know when you are "done." Attach timelines and measurement to goals so that effort leads to defined progress and tangible outcomes.

- ❏ Remember to build celebration and recognition into your life. Achievers tend to move on to the next challenge without acknowledging their successes. Counter this impulse by creating regular opportunities to enjoy your progress and accomplishments.

- ❏ Your drive for action might cause you to find meetings a bit boring. If that's the case, appeal to your Achiever talents by learning the objectives of each meeting ahead of time and by taking notes about progress toward those objectives during the meeting. You can help ensure that meetings are productive and efficient.

- ❏ Continue your education by attaining certifications in your area or specialty in addition to attending conferences and other programs. This will give you even more goals to achieve and will push your existing boundaries of accomplishment.

- ❏ You do not require much motivation from others. Take advantage of your self-motivation by setting challenging goals. Set a more demanding goal every time you finish a project.

- ❏ Partner with other hard workers. Share your goals with them so they can help you get more done.

- ❏ Count personal achievements in your scoring "system." This will help you direct your Achiever talents toward family and friends as well as toward work.

- More work excites you. The prospect of what lies ahead is infinitely more motivating than what has been completed. Launch initiatives and new projects. Your seemingly endless reserve of energy will create enthusiasm and momentum.

- Make sure that in your eagerness to do more at work, you do not skimp on quality. Create measurable outcome standards to guarantee that increased productivity is matched by enhanced quality.

Working With Others Who Have Achiever

- Establish a relationship with Achievers by working alongside them. Working hard together is often a bonding experience for them. They are annoyed by "slackers."

- Recognize that people with Achiever like to be busy. Sitting in meetings is likely to be very boring for them. So only invite them to meetings where you really need them and where they can be fully engaged. If they don't need to be at the meeting, let them get their work done instead.

- Achievers may well need less sleep and get up earlier than others. Look to them when these conditions are required on the job. Also, ask them questions such as "How late did you have to work to get this done?" or "When did you come in this morning?" They will appreciate this kind of attention.

ACTIVATOR

"When can we start?" This is a recurring question in your life. You are impatient for action. You may concede that analysis has its uses or that debate and discussion can occasionally yield some valuable insights, but deep down you know that only action is real. Only action can make things happen. Only action leads to performance. Once a decision is made, you cannot not act. Others may worry that "there are still some things we don't know," but this doesn't seem to slow you. If the decision has been made to go across town, you know that the fastest way to get there is to go stoplight to stoplight. You are not going to sit around waiting until all the lights have turned green. Besides, in your view, action and thinking are not opposites. In fact, guided by your Activator theme, you believe that action is the best device for learning. You make a decision, you take action, you look at the result and you learn. This learning informs your next action and your next. How can you grow if you have nothing to react to? Well, you believe you can't. You must put yourself out there. You must take the next step. It is the only way to keep your thinking fresh and informed. The bottom line is this: You know you will be judged not by what you say, not by what you think, but by what you get done. This does not frighten you. It pleases you.

Activator Sounds Like This:

Jane C., Benedictine nun: "When I was prioress in the 1970s, we were hit by the energy shortage, and costs skyrocketed. We had a hundred and forty acres, and I walked the acreage every day pondering what we should do about this energy shortage. Suddenly I decided that if we had that much land, we should be drilling our own gas well, and so we did. We spent one hundred thousand dollars to drill a gas well. If you have never drilled a gas well, you probably don't realize what I didn't realize: namely, that you have to spend seventy thousand dollars just to drill to see if you have any gas on your property at all. So they dug down with some kind of vibratory camera thing, and they told me that I had a gas pool. But they didn't know how large the pool was, and they didn't know if there was enough pressure to bring it up. 'If you pay another thirty thousand dollars, we will try to release the well,' they said. 'If you don't want us to, we'll just cap the well, take your seventy thousand and go home.' So I gave them the final thirty thousand and, fortunately, up it came. That was twenty years ago, and it is still pumping."

Jim L., entrepreneur: "Some people see my impatience as not wanting to listen to the traps, the potential roadblocks. What I keep repeating is, 'I want to know when I am going to hit the wall, and I need you to tell me how much it is going to hurt. But if I choose to bump into the wall anyway, then don't worry — you've done your job. I just had to experience it for myself.'"

Ideas for Action

- ❏ Seek work in which you can make your own decisions and act on them. In particular, look for start-up or turnaround situations.

- ❏ At work, make sure that your manager judges you on measurable outcomes rather than your process. Your process is not always pretty.

- You can transform innovative ideas into immediate action. Look for creative and original thinkers, and help them move their ideas from conceptual theory to concrete practice.

  Activator

- Look for areas that are bogged down by discussion or blocked by barriers. End the stalemate by creating a plan to get things moving and spur others into action.

- You learn more from real experience than from theoretical discussions. To grow, consciously expose yourself to challenging experiences that will test your talents, skills and knowledge.

- Remember that although your tenacity is powerful, it may intimidate some. Your Activator talents will be most effective when you have first earned others' trust and loyalty.

- Identify the most influential decision-makers in your organization. Make it a point to have lunch with each of them at least once a quarter to share your ideas. They can support you in your activation and provide critical resources to make your ideas happen.

- You can easily energize the plans and ideas of others. Consider partnering with focused, futuristic, strategic or analytical people who will lend their direction and planning to your activation, thereby creating an opportunity to build consensus and get others behind the plan. By doing this, you complement each other.

- Give the reasons why your requests for action must be granted. Otherwise, others might dismiss you as impatient and label you a "ready, fire, aim" person.

- You possess an ability to create motion and momentum in others. Be strategic and wise in the use of your Activator talents. When is the best time, where is the best place and who are the best people with whom to leverage your valuable influence?

Working With Others Who Have Activator

- Tell people with Activator that you know they can make things happen and that you may be asking them for help at key times. Your expectations will energize them.

- When Activators complain, listen carefully — you may learn something. Then get them on your side by talking about new initiatives that they can lead or new improvements that they can make. Do this immediately, because unchecked, they can quickly stir up negativity when they get off track.

- Ask people with Activator what new goals or improvements your team needs to achieve. Then help them see what steps they can take to start making progress toward these goals.

ADAPTABILITY

You live in the moment. You don't see the future as a fixed destination. Instead, you see it as a place that you create out of the choices that you make right now. And so you discover your future one choice at a time. This doesn't mean that you don't have plans. You probably do. But this theme of Adaptability does enable you to respond willingly to the demands of the moment even if they pull you away from your plans. Unlike some, you don't resent sudden requests or unforeseen detours. You expect them. They are inevitable. Indeed, on some level you actually look forward to them. You are, at heart, a very flexible person who can stay productive when the demands of work are pulling you in many different directions at once.

Adaptability Sounds Like This:

Marie T., television producer: "I love live TV because you never know what is going to happen. One minute, I might be putting together a segment on the best teenage holiday gifts, and the next, I will be doing the pre-interview for a presidential candidate. I guess I have always been this way. I live in the moment. If someone asks me, 'What are you doing tomorrow?' my answer is always, 'Hell, I don't know. Depends what I'm in the mood for.' I drive my boyfriend crazy because he'll plan for us to go to the antique market on Sunday afternoon, and then right at the last minute, I'll change my mind and say, 'Nah, let's go home and read the Sunday papers.' Annoying, right? Yeah, but on the positive side, it does mean that I'm up for anything."

Linda G., project manager: "Where I work, I am the calmest person I know. When someone comes in and says, 'We didn't plan right. We need this turned around by tomorrow,' my colleagues seem to tense up and freeze. Somehow that doesn't happen to me. I like that pressure, that need for instant response. It makes me feel alive."

Peter F., corporate trainer: "I think I deal with life better than most people. Last week, I found that my car window had been smashed and the stereo stolen. I was annoyed, of course, but it didn't throw me off my day one bit. I just cleared it, mentally moved on, and went right on with the other things I had to get done that day."

Ideas for Action

- Cultivate your reputation as a calm and reassuring person when others become upset by daily events.

- Avoid roles that demand structure and predictability. These roles will quickly frustrate you, make you feel inadequate and stifle your independence.

- When the pressure is on, help your hesitant friends, colleagues and clients find ways to collect themselves and take control of the situation. Explain that adaptability is about more than simply rolling with the punches; it is about calmly, intelligently and readily responding to circumstances.

- Don't let others abuse your inherent flexibility. Though your Adaptability talents serve you well, don't compromise your long-term success by bending to every whim, desire and demand of others. Use smart guidelines to help you decide when to flex and when to stand firm.

Adaptability

- Seek roles in which success depends on responding to constantly changing circumstances. Consider career areas such as journalism, live television production, emergency healthcare and customer service. In these roles, the best react the fastest and stay levelheaded.

- Fine-tune your responsiveness. For example, if your job demands unanticipated travel, learn how to pack and leave in 30 minutes. If your work pressure comes in unpredictable spurts, practice the first three moves you will always make when the pressure hits.

- Look to others for planning. People who have strong Focus, Strategic or Belief talents can help you shape your long-term goals, leaving you to excel at dealing with the day-to-day variations.

- Your Adaptability talents give you an even-keel mindset that lets you ride the ups and downs without becoming an emotional volcano. Your "don't cry over spilled milk" approach will help you quickly recover from setbacks. Recognize this aspect of your nature, and help your friends and colleagues understand that it is productive flexibility rather than an "I don't care" attitude.

- Avoid tasks that are too structured and that stifle your need for variety. If given a list of tasks to complete, try to indulge your desire for flexibility by making a game of that list. See if you can be creative or make the tasks more fun in some way.

- Openly use your reassuring demeanor to soothe disgruntled friends or coworkers. Think about the approach you used, and remember to apply it again when the situation presents itself.

Working With Others Who Have Adaptability

- People with Adaptability have an instinctively flexible nature that makes them a valuable addition to almost any team. When plans go awry, they will adjust to the new circumstances and try to make progress. They will not sit on the sidelines and sulk.

- With their willingness to "go with the flow," people with Adaptability can provide a wonderful environment in which others can experiment and learn.

- People with Adaptability will be most productive on short-term assignments that require immediate action. They prefer a life filled with many quick skirmishes rather than long, drawn-out campaigns.

ANALYTICAL

Your Analytical theme challenges other people: "Prove it. Show me why what you are claiming is true." In the face of this kind of questioning some will find that their brilliant theories wither and die. For you, this is precisely the point. You do not necessarily want to destroy other people's ideas, but you do insist that their theories be sound. You see yourself as objective and dispassionate. You like data because they are value free. They have no agenda. Armed with these data, you search for patterns and connections. You want to understand how certain patterns affect one another. How do they combine? What is their outcome? Does this outcome fit with the theory being offered or the situation being confronted? These are your questions. You peel the layers back until, gradually, the root cause or causes are revealed. Others see you as logical and rigorous. Over time they will come to you in order to expose someone's "wishful thinking" or "clumsy thinking" to your refining mind. It is hoped that your analysis is never delivered too harshly. Otherwise, others may avoid you when that "wishful thinking" is their own.

Analytical Sounds Like This:

Jose G., school system administrator: "I have an innate ability to see structures, formats and patterns before they exist. For instance, when people are talking about writing a grant proposal, while I'm listening to them, my brain instinctively processes the type of grants that are available and how the discussion fits into the eligibility, right down to the format of how the information can fit on the grant form in a clear and convincing way."

Jack T., human resources executive: "If I make a claim, I need to know that I can back it up with facts and logical thinking. For example, if someone says that our company is not paying as much as other companies, I always ask, 'Why do you say that?' If they say, 'Well, I saw an ad in the paper that offers graduates in mechanical engineering five grand more than we are paying,' I'll reply by asking, 'But where are these graduates going to work? Is their salary based on geography? What types of companies are they going for? Are they manufacturing companies like ours? And how many people are in their sample? Is it three people, and one of them got a really good deal, thus driving the overall average up?' There are many questions I need to ask to ensure that their claim is indeed a fact and not based on one misleading data point."

Leslie J., school principal: "Many times, there are inconsistencies in the performance of the same group of students from one year to the next. It's the same group of kids, but their scores are different year to year. How can this be? Which building are the kids in? How many of the kids have been enrolled for a full academic year? Which teachers were they assigned to, and what teaching styles were used by those teachers? I just love asking questions like these to understand what is truly happening."

Ideas for Action

❑ Choose work in which you are paid to analyze data, find patterns or organize ideas. For example, you might excel in marketing, financial or medical research or in database management, editing or risk management.

- Whatever your role, identify credible sources on which you can rely. You are at your best when you have well-researched sources of information and numbers to support your logic. For example, determine the most helpful books, websites or publications that can serve as references.

Analytical

- Your mind is constantly working and producing insightful analysis. Are others aware of that? Find the best way of expressing your thoughts: writing, one-on-one conversations, group discussions, perhaps lectures or presentations. Put value to your thoughts by communicating them.

- Make sure that your accumulation and analysis of information always leads to its application and implementation. If you don't do this naturally, find a partner who pushes you from theory to practice, from thinking to doing. This person will help ensure that your analysis doesn't turn into paralysis.

- Take an academic course that will expand your Analytical talents. Specifically, study people whose logic you admire.

- Volunteer your Analytical talents. You can be particularly helpful to those who are struggling to organize large quantities of data or having a hard time bringing structure to their ideas.

- Partner with someone with strong Activator talents. This person's impatience will move you more quickly through the analytical phase into the action phase.

- You may remain skeptical until you see solid proof. Your skepticism ensures validity, but others may take it personally. Help others realize that your skepticism is primarily about data, not people.

- Look for patterns in data. See if you can discern a motif, precedent or relationship in scores or numbers. By connecting the dots in the data and inferring a causal link, you may be able to help others see these patterns.

- Help others understand that your analytical approach will often require data and other information to logically back up new ideas that they might suggest.

Working With Others Who Have Analytical

- Whenever people with Analytical are involved in an important decision, take time to think through the issues with them. They will want to know all the key factors involved.

- When you are defending a decision or a principle, show people who have Analytical the supporting numbers. They instinctively give more credibility to information that displays numbers.

- Because accuracy is so important to people with Analytical, getting a task done correctly may be more important to them than meeting a deadline. Therefore, as the deadline draws near, keep checking in with them to make sure that they have the necessary time to do the job right.

ARRANGER

You are a conductor. When faced with a complex situation involving many factors, you enjoy managing all of the variables, aligning and realigning them until you are sure you have arranged them in the most productive configuration possible. In your mind there is nothing special about what you are doing. You are simply trying to figure out the best way to get things done. But others, lacking this theme, will be in awe of your ability. "How can you keep so many things in your head at once?" they will ask. "How can you stay so flexible, so willing to shelve well-laid plans in favor of some brand-new configuration that has just occurred to you?" But you cannot imagine behaving in any other way. You are a shining example of effective flexibility, whether you are changing travel schedules at the last minute because a better fare has popped up or mulling over just the right combination of people and resources to accomplish a new project. From the mundane to the complex, you are always looking for the perfect configuration. Of course, you are at your best in dynamic situations. Confronted with the unexpected, some complain that plans devised with such care cannot be changed, while others take refuge in the existing rules or procedures. You don't do either. Instead, you jump into the confusion, devising new options, hunting for new paths of least resistance and figuring out new partnerships — because, after all, there might just be a better way.

Arranger Sounds Like This:

Sarah P., finance executive: "I love really complicated challenges where I have to think on my feet and figure out how all the pieces fit together. Some people look at a situation, see thirty variables and get hung up trying to balance all thirty. When I look at the same situation, I see about three options. And because I see only three, it's easier for me to make a decision and then put everything into place."

Grant D., operations manager: "I got a message the other day from our manufacturing facility saying that demand for one of our products had greatly exceeded the forecast. I thought about it for a moment, and then an idea popped into my head: Ship the product weekly, not monthly. So I said, 'Let's contact our European subsidiaries, ask them what their demand is, tell them the situation we are in and then ask what their weekly demand is.' That way we can meet requirements without building up our inventory. Sure, it'll drive shipping costs up, but that's better than having too much inventory in one place and not enough in another."

Jane B., entrepreneur: "Sometimes, for instance, when we are all going to a movie or a football game, this Arranger theme drives me up the wall. My family and friends come to rely on me — 'Jane will get the tickets; Jane will organize the transportation.' Why should I always have to do it? But they just say, 'Because you do it well. For us, it would take half an hour. For you, it seems to go much faster. You just call up the ticket place, order the right tickets, and just like that, it's done.'"

Ideas for Action

❑ Learn the goals of your coworkers and friends. Let them know that you are aware of their goals, and then help set them up for success.

Arranger

- ❏ If a team needs to be created, make sure you are involved. You recognize talents, skills and knowledge in people, and that awareness will help you get the right people in the right spots.

- ❏ You intuitively sense how very different people can work together. Take a close look at groups with divergent personalities and opinions, as they may have the greatest need for your Arranger talents.

- ❏ Be sure to keep track of ongoing deadlines for your many tasks, projects and obligations. Although you enjoy the chance to juggle lots of activities, others with less powerful Arranger talents may become anxious if they don't see you working on their projects frequently. Inform them of your progress to ease their fears.

- ❏ Seek complex, dynamic environments in which there are few routines.

- ❏ Take on the organization of a big event — a convention, a large party or a company celebration.

- ❏ Give people time to understand your way of doing things when you present it to them. Your mental juggling is instinctive, but others might find it difficult to break with existing procedures. Take the time to clearly explain why your way can be more effective.

- ❏ At work, focus your Arranger talents on the most dynamic areas of your organization. Divisions or departments that are static and routine in nature are likely to bore you. You will thrive when your Arranger talents are energized, and you will suffer when you are bored.

- Help others see your far-reaching expertise by sharing your "what if" thinking with them. When they know you've identified and carefully considered all possible options and arrangements, they'll feel more confident.

- You are flexible in the way you organize people as well as in how you configure space. Figure out how you can improve workflow by rearranging spaces and/or procedures to maximize efficiency and to free up time for yourself and for others.

Working With Others Who Have Arranger

- People with Arranger are excited by complex, multifaceted assignments. They will thrive in situations in which they have many things going on at the same time.

- When you are launching a project, ask Arrangers for help positioning the members of the project team. They are good at figuring out how each person's strengths might add the greatest value to the team.

- People who have Arranger can be resourceful. Feel confident that if something is not working, they will enjoy figuring out other ways to do things.

BELIEF

If you possess a strong Belief theme, you have certain core values that are enduring. These values vary from one person to another, but ordinarily your Belief theme causes you to be family-oriented, altruistic, even spiritual, and to value responsibility and high ethics — both in yourself and others. These core values affect your behavior in many ways. They give your life meaning and satisfaction; in your view, success is more than money and prestige. They provide you with direction, guiding you through the temptations and distractions of life toward a consistent set of priorities. This consistency is the foundation for all your relationships. Your friends call you dependable. "I know where you stand," they say. Your Belief makes you easy to trust. It also demands that you find work that meshes with your values. Your work must be meaningful; it must matter to you. And guided by your Belief theme it will matter only if it gives you a chance to live out your values.

Belief Sounds Like This:

Michael K., salesperson: "The vast majority of my nonworking time goes to my family and to the things we do in the community. I was on the countywide Boy Scouts board of directors. And when I was a Boy Scout, I was pack leader. When I was an Explorer, I was junior assistant leader for the Boy Scouts. I just like being with kids. I believe that's where the future is. And I think you can do a whole lot worse with your time than investing it in the future."

Lara M., college president: "My values are why I work so hard every day at my job. I put hours and hours into this job, and I don't even care what I get paid. I just found out that I am the lowest paid college president in my state, and I don't even care. I mean, I don't do this for the money."

Tracy D., airline executive: "If you are not doing something important, why bother? Getting up every day and working on ways to make flying safer seems important to me, purposeful. If I didn't find this purpose in my job, I don't know if I could work through all the challenges and frustrations that get in my way. I think I would get demoralized."

Ideas for Action

- ❏ Clarify your values by thinking about one of your best days ever. How did your values play into the satisfaction that you received on that day? How can you organize your life to repeat that day as often as possible?

- ❏ Actively seek roles that fit your values. In particular, think about joining organizations that define their purpose by the contribution they make to society.

- ❏ The meaning and purpose of your work will often provide direction for others. Remind people why their work is important and how it makes a difference in their lives and in the lives of others.

- ❏ Your Belief talents allow you to talk to the hearts of people. Develop a "purpose statement," and communicate it to your family, friends and coworkers. Your powerful emotional appeal can give them a motivating sense of contribution.

❏ Create a gallery of letters and/or pictures of the people whose lives you have substantially influenced. When you are feeling down or overwhelmed, remind yourself of your value by looking at this gallery. It will energize you and revive your commitment to helping others.

❏ Set aside time to ensure that you are balancing your work demands and your personal life. Your devotion to your career should not come at the expense of your strong commitment to your family.

❏ Don't be afraid to give voice to your values. This will help others know who you are and how to relate to you.

❏ Actively cultivate friends who share your basic values. Consider your best friend. Does this person share your value system?

❏ Partner with someone who has strong Futuristic talents. This person can energize you by painting a vivid picture of the direction in which your values will lead.

❏ Accept that the values of other people might differ from your own. Express your beliefs without being judgmental.

Working With Others Who Have Belief

❏ People with Belief are likely to be very passionate about the things closest to their heart. Discover that passion, and help them connect it to the work they have to do.

- When working with people who have Belief, learn about their family and community. They will have made rock-solid commitments to those who are important to them. Understand, appreciate and honor these commitments, and they will respect you for it.

- You do not need to have the same belief system that people with Belief do, but you do have to understand it, respect it and apply it. Otherwise, major conflicts will eventually erupt.

COMMAND

Command leads you to take charge. Unlike some people, you feel no discomfort with imposing your views on others. On the contrary, once your opinion is formed, you need to share it with others. Once your goal is set, you feel restless until you have aligned others with you. You are not frightened by confrontation; rather, you know that confrontation is the first step toward resolution. Whereas others may avoid facing up to life's unpleasantness, you feel compelled to present the facts or the truth, no matter how unpleasant it may be. You need things to be clear between people and challenge them to be clear-eyed and honest. You push them to take risks. You may even intimidate them. And while some may resent this, labeling you opinionated, they often willingly hand you the reins. People are drawn toward those who take a stance and ask them to move in a certain direction. Therefore, people will be drawn to you. You have presence. You have Command.

Command Sounds Like This:

Malcolm M., hospitality manager: "One reason I affect people is that I am so candid. Actually, people say that I intimidate them at first. After I work with them a year, we talk about that sometimes. They say, 'Boy, Malcolm, when I started working here, I was scared to death.' When I ask why, they say, 'I've never worked with anyone who just said it. Whatever it was, whatever needed to be said, you just said it.'"

Rick P., retail executive: "We have a wellness program whereby if you consume less than four alcoholic beverages a week, you get twenty-five dollars; if you don't smoke, you get twenty-five dollars a month. So one day I got word that one of my store managers was smoking again. This was not good. He was smoking in the store, setting a bad example for the employees and claiming his twenty-five dollars. I just can't keep stuff like that inside. It wasn't comfortable, but I confronted him with it immediately and clearly: 'Stop doing that, or you are fired.' He's basically a good guy, but you can't let things like that slide."

Diane N., hospice worker: "I don't think of myself as assertive, but I do take charge. When you walk into a room with a dying person and their family, you have to take charge. They want you to take charge. They are a bit in shock, a bit frightened, a bit in denial. Basically, they're confused. They need someone to tell them what is going to happen next, what they can expect — that it's not going to be fun but that in some important ways, it will be all right. They don't want mousy and soft. They want clarity and honesty. I provide it."

Ideas for Action

- ❑ You will always be ready to confront. Practice the words, the tone and the techniques that will turn your ability to confront into real persuasiveness.

- ❑ In your relationships, seize opportunities to speak plainly and directly about sensitive subjects. Your unwillingness to hide from the truth can become a source of strength and constancy for your colleagues and friends. Strive to become known as a candid person.

- ❑ Ask people for their opinions. Sometimes your candor will be intimidating, causing others to tread lightly for fear of your reaction. Watch for this. If necessary, explain that you are upfront simply because it feels uncomfortable to keep things bottled up, not because you want to frighten other people into silence.

☐ Partner with someone with strong Woo or Empathy talents. Some obstacles do not need to be confronted; they can be circumvented. This person can help you avoid obstacles through relationships.

Command

☐ Your "take charge" attitude steadies and reassures others in times of crisis. When faced with a particularly trying challenge, use your Command talents to assuage others' fears and convince them you have things under control.

☐ Your Command talents might compel you to wrestle for the reins of power because you love being in the driver's seat. But remember that even when you are not formally in charge, your presence can be an unseen yet powerfully felt force.

☐ Step up and break bottlenecks. Others count on your natural decisiveness to get things moving. When you remove roadblocks, you often create new momentum and success that would not have existed without you.

☐ Consider taking the lead on a committee. You have definite ideas about what you would like to see happen, and you can naturally influence a group to follow you. You might be comfortable spearheading new initiatives.

☐ Seek roles in which you will be asked to persuade others. Consider whether selling would be a good career for you.

☐ Find a cause you believe in, and support it. You might discover yourself at your best when defending a cause in the face of resistance.

Working With Others Who Have Command

- Always ask people with Command for an evaluation of what's happening in your organization. They are likely to give you a straight answer. In the same vein, look to them to raise ideas that are different from your own. They aren't likely to be head-nodders.

- When you need to jar a project loose and get things moving again, or when people need to be persuaded, look to people who have Command to take charge.

- Never threaten people who have Command unless you are 100% ready to follow through.

COMMUNICATION

You like to explain, to describe, to host, to speak in public and to write. This is your Communication theme at work. Ideas are a dry beginning. Events are static. You feel a need to bring them to life, to energize them, to make them exciting and vivid. And so you turn events into stories and practice telling them. You take the dry idea and enliven it with images and examples and metaphors. You believe that most people have a very short attention span. They are bombarded by information, but very little of it survives. You want your information — whether an idea, an event, a product's features and benefits, a discovery, or a lesson — to survive. You want to divert their attention toward you and then capture it, lock it in. This is what drives your hunt for the perfect phrase. This is what draws you toward dramatic words and powerful word combinations. This is why people like to listen to you. Your word pictures pique their interest, sharpen their world and inspire them to act.

Communication Sounds Like This:

Sheila K., general manager of a theme park: "Stories are the best way to make my point. Yesterday I wanted to show my executive committee the impact we can have on our guests, so I shared this story with them: One of our employees brought her father to the flag-raising ceremony we have for Veterans Day here at the theme park. He was disabled during World War II, and he now has a rare form of cancer and has had a lot of surgery. He's dying. At the start of the ceremony, one of our employees said to the group, 'This man is a World War II veteran. Can we give him a hand?' Everybody cheered, and his daughter started crying. Her dad took off his hat. He never takes off his hat because of the scars on his head from the war and the cancer surgery, but when the national anthem started, he took off his hat and bowed his head. His daughter told me later that it was the best day he's had in years."

Tom P., banking executive: "My most recent client thought that the flow of capital toward internet stocks was just a passing phase. I tried using a rational argument to change his mind, but he couldn't or wouldn't be convinced. In the end, as I often do when faced with a client in denial, I resorted to imagery. I told him that he was like a person sitting on a beach with his back to the sea. The internet was like a fast-rising tide. No matter how comfortable he felt right now, the tide was rising with each crashing wave, and very soon, one of those waves would come crashing down over his head and engulf him. He got the point."

Margret D., marketing director: "I once read a book about giving speeches that gave two suggestions: Talk only about things you're really passionate about, and always use personal examples. I immediately started doing that, and I found lots of stories because I have kids and grandkids and a husband. I build my stories around my personal experiences because everyone can relate to them."

Ideas for Action

❑ You will always do well in roles that require you to capture people's attention. Think about a career in teaching, sales, marketing, ministry or the media. Your Communication talents are likely to flourish in these areas.

❑ Start a collection of stories or phrases that resonate with you. For example, cut out magazine articles that move you, or write down powerful word combinations. Practice telling these stories or saying these words out loud, by yourself. Listen to yourself actually saying the words. Refine.

❑ When you are presenting, pay close attention to your audience. Watch their reactions to each part of your presentation. You will notice that some parts are especially engaging. Afterward, take time to identify the moments that particularly caught the audience's attention. Draft your next presentation around these highlights.

❑ Practice. Improvisation has a certain appeal, but in general, an audience will respond best to presenters who know where they are headed. Counterintuitively, the more prepared you are, the more natural your improvisations will appear.

❑ Identify your most beneficial sounding boards and audiences — the listeners who seem to bring out your best communication. Examine these individuals or groups to learn why you are so good when you speak with them or to them, and look for the same qualities in potential partners and audiences.

❑ Keep getting smarter about the words you use. They are a critical currency. Spend them wisely, and monitor their impact.

❑ Your Communication talents can be highly effective when your message has substance. Don't rely on your talents alone; take your communication to the level of strength by developing your knowledge and expertise in specific areas.

- ❏ You are gifted at fostering dialogue among peers and colleagues. Use your Communication talents to summarize the various points in a meeting and to build consensus by helping others see what they have in common.

- ❏ If you enjoy writing, consider publishing your work. If you enjoy public speaking, make a presentation at a professional meeting or convention. In either case, your Communication talents will serve to assist you in finding just the right way to frame your ideas and state your purpose. You delight in sharing your thoughts with others, so find the medium that best fits your voice and message.

- ❏ Volunteer for opportunities to present. You can become known as someone who helps people express their thoughts and ambitions in a captivating way.

Working With Others Who Have Communication

- ❏ People with Communication find it easy to carry on a conversation. Ask them to come to social gatherings, dinners or any events where you want to entertain prospects or customers.

- ❏ When you work with people who have Communication, take the time to hear about their life and experiences. They will enjoy telling you, and you will enjoy listening. And your relationship will be closer because of it.

- ❏ Discuss plans for your organization's social events with people who have Communication. They are likely to have good ideas — both for entertainment and for what should be communicated at the event.

COMPETITION

Competition is rooted in comparison. When you look at the world, you are instinctively aware of other people's performance. Their performance is the ultimate yardstick. No matter how hard you tried, no matter how worthy your intentions, if you reached your goal but did not outperform your peers, the achievement feels hollow. Like all competitors, you need other people. You need to compare. If you can compare, you can compete, and if you can compete, you can win. And when you win, there is no feeling quite like it. You like measurement because it facilitates comparisons. You like other competitors because they invigorate you. You like contests because they must produce a winner. You particularly like contests where you know you have the inside track to be the winner. Although you are gracious to your fellow competitors and even stoic in defeat, you don't compete for the fun of competing. You compete to win. Over time you will come to avoid contests where winning seems unlikely.

Competition Sounds Like This:

Mark L., sales executive: "I've played sports my entire life, and I don't just play to have fun — let me put it that way. I like to engage in sports I am going to win and not ones I am going to lose, because if I lose, I am outwardly gracious but inwardly infuriated."

Harry D., general manager: "I'm not a big sailor, but I love the America's Cup. Both boats are supposed to be exactly the same, and both crews have top-notch athletes. But you always get a winner. One of them had some secret up their sleeves that tipped the balance and enabled them to win more often than lose. And that's what I am looking for — that secret, that tiny edge."

Sumner Redstone, chairman of Viacom (now known as CBS Corporation), on his efforts to acquire that company: "I relished every minute of it because Viacom was a company worth fighting for, and I enjoyed a contest. If you get involved in a major competitive struggle and the stress that inevitably comes with it, you'd better derive some real sense of satisfaction and enjoyment from the ultimate victory. Wrestling control of a company like Viacom was warfare. I believe the real lesson it taught me was that it is not about money, it's about the will to win."

Ideas for Action

- ❏ Select work environments in which you can measure your achievements. You might not be able to discover how good you can be without competing.

- ❏ List the performance scores that help you know where you stand every day. What scores should you pay attention to?

- ❏ Identify a high-achieving person against whom you can measure your own achievement. If there is more than one, list all the people with whom you currently compete. Without measurement, how will you know if you won?

- ❏ Try to turn ordinary tasks into competitive games. You will get more done this way.

- ❏ When you win, take the time to investigate why you won. You can learn a great deal more from a victory than from a loss.

- Let people know that being competitive does not equate with putting others down. Explain that you derive satisfaction from pitting yourself against good, strong competitors and winning.

- Develop a "balanced metric"— a measurement system that will monitor all aspects of your performance. Even if you are competing against your own previous numbers, this measurement will help you give proper attention to all aspects of your performance.

- When competing with others, create development opportunities by choosing to compare yourself with someone who is slightly above your current level of expertise. Your competition will push you to refine your skills and knowledge to exceed those of that person. Look one or two levels above you for a role model who will push you to improve.

- Take the time to celebrate your wins. In your world, there is no victory without celebration.

- Design some mental strategies that can help you deal with a loss. Armed with these strategies, you will be able to move on to the next challenge much more quickly.

Working With Others Who Have Competition

- Use competitive language with people who have Competition. It is a win-lose world for them, so from their perspective, achieving a goal is winning, and missing a goal is losing.

- ❏ Help people with Competition find places where they can win. If they lose repeatedly, they may stop playing. Remember, in the contests that matter to them, they don't compete for the fun of it. They compete to win.

- ❏ When people with Competition lose, they may need to mourn for a while. Let them. Then help them quickly move into another opportunity to win.

CONNECTEDNESS

Things happen for a reason. You are sure of it. You are sure of it because in your soul you know that we are all connected. Yes, we are individuals, responsible for our own judgments and in possession of our own free will, but nonetheless we are part of something larger. Some may call it the collective unconscious. Others may label it spirit or life force. But whatever your word of choice, you gain confidence from knowing that we are not isolated from one another or from the earth and the life on it. This feeling of Connectedness implies certain responsibilities. If we are all part of a larger picture, then we must not harm others because we will be harming ourselves. We must not exploit because we will be exploiting ourselves. Your awareness of these responsibilities creates your value system. You are considerate, caring and accepting. Certain of the unity of humankind, you are a bridge builder for people of different cultures. Sensitive to the invisible hand, you can give others comfort that there is a purpose beyond our humdrum lives. The exact articles of your faith will depend on your upbringing and your culture, but your faith is strong. It sustains you and your close friends in the face of life's mysteries.

Connectedness Sounds Like This:

Mandy M., homemaker: "Humility is the essence of Connectedness. You have to know who you are and who you aren't. I have a piece of the wisdom. I don't have much of it, but what I do have is real. This isn't grandiosity. This is real humility. You have confidence in your gifts, real confidence, but you know you don't have all the answers. You start to feel connected to others because you know they have wisdom that you don't. You can't feel connected if you think you have everything."

Rose T., psychologist: "Sometimes I look at my bowl of cereal in the morning and think about those hundreds of people who were involved in bringing me my bowl of cereal: the farmers in the field, the biochemists who made the pesticides, the warehouse workers at the food preparation plants, even the marketers who somehow persuaded me to buy this box of cereal and not a different one sitting next to it on the shelf. I know it sounds strange, but I give thanks to these people, and just doing that makes me feel more involved with life, more connected to things, less alone."

Chuck M., teacher: "I tend to be very black and white about things, but when it comes to understanding the mysteries of life, for some reason, I am much more open. I have a big interest in learning about all different religions. I am reading a book right now that talks about Judaism versus Christianity versus the religion of the Canaanites. Buddhism, Greek mythology — it's really interesting how all of these tie together in some way."

Ideas for Action

- ❑ Consider roles in which you listen and counsel. You can become adept at helping other people see connection and purpose in everyday occurrences.

- ❑ Explore specific ways to expand your sense of connection, such as starting a book club, attending a retreat or joining an organization that puts Connectedness into practice.

- Within your organization, help your colleagues understand how their efforts fit in the larger picture. You can be a leader in building teams and helping people feel important.

- You are aware of the boundaries and borders created within organizations and communities, but you treat them as seamless and fluid. Use your Connectedness talents to break down silos that prevent shared knowledge.

Connectedness

- Help people see the connections among their talents, their actions, their mission and their successes. When people believe in what they are doing and feel like they are part of something bigger, their commitment to achievement is enhanced.

- Partner with someone with strong Communication talents. This person can help you with the words you need to describe vivid examples of connection in the real world.

- Don't spend too much time attempting to persuade others to see the world as a linked web. Be aware that your sense of connection is intuitive. If others don't share your intuition, rational argument will not persuade them.

- Your philosophy of life compels you to move beyond your own self-interests and the interests of your immediate constituency and sphere of influence. As such, you see the broader implications for your community and the world. Explore ways to communicate these insights to others.

- Seek out global or cross-cultural responsibilities that capitalize on your understanding of the commonalities inherent in humanity. Build universal capability, and change the mindset of those who think in terms of "us" and "them."

- ❏ Connectedness talents can help you look past someone's outer shell to embrace their humanity. Be particularly aware of this when you work with somebody whose background is very different from yours. You can naturally look past the labels and focus on their essential needs.

Working With Others Who Have Connectedness

- ❏ People with Connectedness will likely have social issues that they will defend strongly. Listen closely to know what inspires this passion. Your acceptance of these issues will influence the depth of the relationship you can build with them.

- ❏ Encourage people with Connectedness to build bridges to the different groups in your organization. They naturally think about how things are connected, so they should excel at showing different people how everyone relies on each other.

- ❏ If you also have dominant Connectedness talents, share articles, writings and experiences with people who have Connectedness. You can reinforce each other's focus.

CONSISTENCY

Balance is important to you. You are keenly aware of the need to treat people the same, no matter what their station in life, so you do not want to see the scales tipped too far in any one person's favor. In your view this leads to selfishness and individualism. It leads to a world where some people gain an unfair advantage because of their connections or their background or their greasing of the wheels. This is truly offensive to you. You see yourself as a guardian against it. In direct contrast to this world of special favors, you believe that people function best in a consistent environment where the rules are clear and are applied to everyone equally. This is an environment where people know what is expected. It is predictable and evenhanded. It is fair. Here each person has an even chance to show their worth.

Consistency Sounds Like This:

Simon H., hotel general manager: "I often remind my senior managers that they shouldn't be abusing their parking privileges or using their position to take golf tee times when there are guests waiting. They hate my drawing attention to this, but I am just the kind of person who dislikes people abusing their perks. I also spend a great deal of time with our hourly employees. I have tremendous respect for them."

Jamie K., magazine editor: "I am the person who always roots for the underdog. I hate it when people don't get a fair shot because of some circumstance in their life that they couldn't control. To put some teeth to this, I am going to set up a scholarship at my alma mater so that journalism students of limited means can do internships in the real world without having to keep paying for their college tuition. I was lucky. When I was an intern in New York at NBC, my family could afford it. Some families can't, but those students should still get a fair shot."

Ben F., operations manager: "Always give credit where credit is due; that's my motto. If I am in a meeting and I bring up an idea that one of my staff actually came up with, I make sure to publicly attribute the idea to that person. Why? Because my bosses always did that with me, and now it seems like the only fair and proper thing to do."

Ideas for Action

- ❏ Make a list of the rules of consistency by which you can live. These rules might be based on certain values that you have or on certain policies that you consider "non-negotiables." Counterintuitively, the clearer you are about these rules, the more comfortable you will be with individuality within these boundaries.

- ❏ Seek roles in which you can be a force for leveling the playing field. At work or in your community, become a leader in helping provide disadvantaged people with the platform they need to show their true potential.

- ❏ Cultivate a reputation for pinpointing those who really deserve credit. Make sure that respect is always given to those who truly performed the work. You can become known as the conscience of your organization or group.

- ❏ Find a role in which you can enforce compliance to a set of standards. Always be ready to challenge people who break the rules or "grease the wheels" to earn an unfair advantage for themselves.

- ❏ Keep your focus on performance. Your Consistency talents might occasionally lead you to overemphasize *how* others get work done and ignore *what* they get done.

- ❏ Because you value equality, you find it hard to deal with individuals who bend the rules to fit their situation. Your Consistency talents can help you clarify rules, policies and procedures in ways that will ensure that they are applied uniformly across the board. Consider drafting protocols to make sure that these rules are clearly stated.

- ❏ Partner with someone with powerful Maximizer or Individualization talents. They can remind you when it is appropriate to accommodate individual differences.

- ❏ Always practice what you preach. This sets the tone for equality and encourages peaceful compliance.

- ❏ Others will appreciate your natural commitment to consistency between what you have promised and what you will deliver. Always stand up for what you believe, even in the face of strong resistance. You will reap long-lasting benefits.

- ❏ Leverage your Consistency talents when you have to communicate "not so pleasant" news. You can be naturally adept at helping others appreciate the rationale behind decisions, which will make the situation easier on them — and you.

Working With Others Who Have Consistency

- ❑ Be supportive of people with Consistency during times of great change because they are most comfortable with predictable patterns that they know work well.

- ❑ People with Consistency have a practical bent and thus will tend to prefer getting tasks accomplished and decisions made rather than doing more abstract work such as brainstorming or long-range planning.

- ❑ When it comes time to recognize others after a project is completed, ask people with Consistency to pinpoint everyone's contributions. They will make sure that each person receives the accolades they truly deserve.

CONTEXT

You look back. You look back because that is where the answers lie. You look back to understand the present. From your vantage point the present is unstable, a confusing clamor of competing voices. It is only by casting your mind back to an earlier time, a time when the plans were being drawn up, that the present regains its stability. The earlier time was a simpler time. It was a time of blueprints. As you look back, you begin to see these blueprints emerge. You realize what the initial intentions were. These blueprints or intentions have since become so embellished that they are almost unrecognizable, but now this Context theme reveals them again. This understanding brings you confidence. No longer disoriented, you make better decisions because you sense the underlying structure. You become a better partner because you understand how your colleagues came to be who they are. And counterintuitively you become wiser about the future because you saw its seeds being sown in the past. Faced with new people and new situations, it will take you a little time to orient yourself, but you must give yourself this time. You must discipline yourself to ask the questions and allow the blueprints to emerge because no matter what the situation, if you haven't seen the blueprints, you will have less confidence in your decisions.

Context Sounds Like This:

Adam Y., software designer: "I tell my people, 'Let's avoid *vuja de*.' And they say, 'Isn't that the wrong word? Shouldn't it be *déjà vu*?' And I say, 'No, *vuja de* means that we're bound to repeat the mistakes of our past. We must avoid this. We must look to our past, see what led to our mistakes, and then not make them again.' It sounds obvious, but most people don't look to their past or don't trust that it was valid or something. And so for them, it's *vuja de* all over again."

Jesse K., media analyst: "I have very little empathy, so I don't relate to people through their present emotional state. Instead, I relate to them through their past. In fact, I can't even begin to understand people until I have found out where they grew up, what their parents were like and what they studied in college."

Gregg H., accounting manager: "I recently moved the whole office to a new accounting system, and the only reason it worked was that I honored their past. When people build an accounting system, it's their blood, sweat and tears; it's *them*. They are personally identified with it. So if I come in and blandly tell them that I'm going to change it, it's like me saying I am going to take your baby away. That's the level of emotion I was dealing with. I had to respect this connection, this history, or they would have rejected me out of hand."

Ideas for Action

- Before planning begins on a project, encourage the people involved to study past projects. Help them appreciate the statement: "Those who cannot remember the past are condemned to repeat it."

- If you are in a role that requires teaching others, build your lessons around case studies. You will enjoy the search for the appropriate case, and your students will learn from these precedents. Use your understanding of the past to help others map the future.

- At work, help your organization strengthen its culture via folklore. For example, collect symbols and stories that represent the best of the past, or suggest naming an award after a person who embodied the historical traditions of your organization.

- Partner with someone with strong Futuristic or Strategic talents. Their fascination with what "could be" will stop you from becoming mired in the past, while your deep understanding of context will stop them from ignoring the lessons of the past. Together you are more likely to create something that lasts.

- Accept change. Remember that your Context talents do not require you to "live in the past." Instead, you can actually become known as an active agent for positive change. Your natural sense of context should allow you to identify more clearly than most the aspects of the past that can be discarded and those that must be retained to build a sustainable future.

- Use fact-based comparisons to prior successes to paint a vivid picture for others of "what can be" in the future. The real-life illustrations you create can build confidence and emotional engagement.

- You recognize that the best predictor of future behavior is past behavior. Probe your friends and coworkers about actions that might have contributed to their current successes so you can help them make better choices in the future. This will help them put their decisions into an overall context.

- ❑ Read historical novels, nonfiction books or biographies. You will discover many insights that will help you understand the present. You will think more clearly.

- ❑ Compare historical antecedents and situations to your current challenges. Identifying commonalities may lead you to a new perspective or an answer to your problems.

- ❑ Seek out mentors who have a sense of history. Listening to their memories is likely to spark your thought process.

Working With Others Who Have Context

- ❑ During meetings, always turn to people with Context to review what's been done and what's been learned. Instinctively, they will want others to be aware of the context of decision-making.

- ❑ People with Context think in terms of case studies: "When did we face a similar situation? What did we do? What happened? What did we learn?" You can expect them to use this talent to help others learn, especially when the need for anecdotes and illustrations is important.

- ❑ When you introduce new colleagues to people with Context, ask them to talk about their backgrounds before you get down to business.

DELIBERATIVE

You are careful. You are vigilant. You are a private person. You know that the world is an unpredictable place. Everything may seem in order, but beneath the surface you sense the many risks. Rather than denying these risks, you draw each one out into the open. Then each risk can be identified, assessed and ultimately reduced. Thus, you are a fairly serious person who approaches life with a certain reserve. For example, you like to plan ahead so as to anticipate what might go wrong. You select your friends cautiously and keep your own counsel when the conversation turns to personal matters. You are careful not to give too much praise and recognition, lest it be misconstrued. If some people don't like you because you are not as effusive as others, then so be it. For you, life is not a popularity contest. Life is something of a minefield. Others can run through it recklessly if they so choose, but you take a different approach. You identify the dangers, weigh their relative impact and then place your feet deliberately. You walk with care.

Deliberative Sounds Like This:

Dick H., film producer: "My whole thing is to reduce the number of variables out there — the fewer the variables, the lower the risk. When I am negotiating with directors, I always start by giving in on some of the smaller points right away. Then once I have taken the smaller issues out of play, I feel better. I can focus. I can control the conversation."

Debbie M., project manager: "I am the practical one. When my colleagues are spouting all of these wonderful ideas, I am asking questions like, 'How is this going to work? How is this going to be accepted by this group or that group of people?'

I won't say that I play devil's advocate, because that is too negative, but I do weigh the implications and assess risk. And I think we all make better decisions because of my questions."

Jamie B., service worker: "I am not a very organized person, but the one thing I do without fail is double-check. I don't do it because I am hyper-responsible or anything. I do it to feel secure. With relationships, with performance, with anything, I am out there on a limb, and I need to know that the particular branch I am standing on is solid."

Brian B., school administrator: "I am putting together a safe-schools plan. I am going to conferences, and we have eight committees working. We have a district-wide review board, but I am still not comfortable with the basic model. My boss asks, 'When can I see the plan?' And I say, 'Not yet. I am not comfortable.' With a big smile on her face, she says, 'Gee, Brian, I don't want it to be perfect, I just want a plan.' But she lets me be because she knows that the care I take now pays big dividends. Because of this pre-work, once the decision is made, it stays made. It doesn't unravel."

Ideas for Action

- You have naturally good judgment, so consider work in which you can provide advice and counsel. You might be especially adept at legal work, crafting sound business deals or ensuring compliance to regulations.

- Whatever your role, take responsibility for helping others think through their decisions. You can see factors that others may not see. You will soon be sought as a valuable sounding board.

- Explain your process of careful decision-making — that you highlight risk in order to take control and reduce it. You don't want others to misconstrue your Deliberative talents for tentativeness or fear of action.

- You inspire trust because you are cautious and considerate about sensitive topics. Use these talents by taking on opportunities to handle delicate issues and conflicts.

- Rather than take foolhardy risks, you are apt to approach a decision cautiously. Trust your instincts when you believe that something is too good to be true.

- During times of change, consider the advantages of being conservative in your decision-making. Be ready to explain these advantages to others.

Deliberative

- Don't let anyone push you into revealing too much about yourself too soon. Check people out carefully before sharing confidential information. You naturally build friendships slowly, so take pride in your small circle of good friends.

- Partner with someone with strong Command, Self-Assurance or Activator talents. Together you will make many decisions, and these decisions will be sound.

- Temper others' tendency to haphazardly move to action by declaring a "consideration" period before decisions are made. Your caution can steer others away from folly and toward wise conclusions.

- Give yourself permission to withhold your opinion until you get all the facts and have an opportunity to ponder your stance. You are not someone who embraces change immediately; you are apt to reflect on possible outcomes so that all the angles are covered. As a deliberative person, you function as a "brake" for more impulsive types who wish to move quickly.

Working With Others Who Have Deliberative

- Ask people with Deliberative to join teams or groups that tend to be impulsive. They will have a temporizing effect, adding much-needed thoughtfulness and anticipation to the mix.

- People with Deliberative are likely to be rigorous thinkers. Before you make a decision, ask them to help you identify the land mines that may derail your plans.

- Respect the fact that people with Deliberative may be private. Unless invited, do not push to become too familiar with them too quickly. And by the same token, don't take it personally if they keep you at arm's length.

DEVELOPER

You see the potential in others. Very often, in fact, potential is all you see. In your view no individual is fully formed. On the contrary, each individual is a work in progress, alive with possibilities. And you are drawn toward people for this very reason. When you interact with others, your goal is to help them experience success. You look for ways to challenge them. You devise interesting experiences that can stretch them and help them grow. And all the while you are on the lookout for the signs of growth — a new behavior learned or modified, a slight improvement in a skill, a glimpse of excellence or of "flow" where previously there were only halting steps. For you these small increments — invisible to some — are clear signs of potential being realized. These signs of growth in others are your fuel. They bring you strength and satisfaction. Over time many will seek you out for help and encouragement because on some level they know that your helpfulness is both genuine and fulfilling to you.

Developer Sounds Like This:

Marilyn K., college president: "At graduation time when a nursing student walks across the stage and gets her diploma, and about 18 rows back some little kid is standing on a chair with a group yelling, 'Yeah, Mom!' — I love that. I cry every time."

John M., advertising executive: "I'm not a lawyer, doctor or candlestick maker. My skills are of a different type. They have to do with understanding people and motives, and the pleasure I get is from watching people discover themselves in ways they never thought possible and from finding people who bring to the table talents that I don't have."

Anna G., nurse: "I had a patient, a young woman, with lung damage so bad that she will have to be on oxygen forever. She will never have the energy or the strength to live a normal life, and I walk in and she's desperate. She doesn't know if she is short of breath because she is anxious or anxious because she is short of breath. And she's talking suicide because she can't work, can't support her husband. So I got her thinking about what she could do rather than what she couldn't. It turns out that she is very creative with arts and crafts, so I told her, 'Look, there are things you can do, and if those things bring you pleasure, then do them. It's a place to start.' And she cried and said, 'I have the energy to wash only one bowl.' I said, 'That's today. Tomorrow you can wash two.' And by Christmas, she was making all kinds of things and selling them too."

Ideas for Action

- ❏ Make a list of the people you have helped learn and grow. Look at the list often, and remind yourself of the effect you have had on the world.

- ❏ Seek roles in which your primary responsibilities include facilitating growth. Teaching, coaching or managing roles might prove especially satisfying for you.

- ❏ Notice when others succeed, and tell them. Be specific about what you saw. Your detailed observations of what led to their victory will enhance their growth.

- Identify the mentor or mentors who recognized something special inside you. Take the time to thank them for helping you develop, even if this means tracking down a former schoolteacher and sending them a letter.

- Partner with someone with strong Individualization talents. They can help you see where each person's greatest talents lie. Without this help, your Developer instincts might lead you to encourage people to grow in areas in which they lack real talent.

- Carefully avoid supporting someone who is consistently struggling in their role. In such instances, the most developmental action you can take is to encourage them to find a different role — a role that fits.

- You will always be compelled to mentor more people than possible. To fulfill this inner drive while maintaining a primary mentoring focus, consider the impact of being a "mentor for the moment." Many of the most poignant and memorable developmental moments occur when the right words are delivered at the right time — words that clarify understanding, reignite a passion, open eyes to an opportunity and change a life course.

- Don't overinvest in losing causes. Your natural inclination to see the best in people and situations can create a blind spot that will keep you from moving on to more opportune situations.

- Your Developer talents might lead you to become so invested in the growth of others that you ignore your own development. Remember that you cannot give what you do not have. If you want to have a bigger impact on the well-being and growth of others, you need to keep growing yourself. Find a mentor or coach who can invest in you.

❑ Make a list of the people you would like to help develop. Write down what you consider to be each person's strengths. Schedule time to meet with each of them regularly — even if for only 15 minutes — and make a point of discussing their goals and their strengths.

Working With Others Who Have Developer

❑ Reinforce Developers' self-concepts as people who encourage others to stretch and to excel. For example, tell them, "Your coworkers would never have broken the record by themselves. Your encouragement and confidence gave them the spark they needed."

❑ Look to people who have Developer when it is time to recognize coworkers. They will enjoy selecting the achievements that deserve praise, and their colleagues on the receiving end will know that the praise is genuine.

❑ Ask people who have Developer to help you grow in your job. They are likely to pick up small increments of progress that others miss.

DISCIPLINE

Your world needs to be predictable. It needs to be ordered and planned. So you instinctively impose structure on your world. You set up routines. You focus on timelines and deadlines. You break long-term projects into a series of specific short-term plans, and you work through each plan diligently. You are not necessarily neat and clean, but you do need precision. Faced with the inherent messiness of life, you want to feel in control. The routines, the timelines, the structure, all of these help create this feeling of control. Lacking this theme of Discipline, others may sometimes resent your need for order, but there need not be conflict. You must understand that not everyone feels your urge for predictability; they have other ways of getting things done. Likewise, you can help them understand and even appreciate your need for structure. Your dislike of surprises, your impatience with errors, your routines and your detail orientation don't need to be misinterpreted as controlling behaviors that box people in. Rather, these behaviors can be understood as your instinctive method for maintaining your progress and your productivity in the face of life's many distractions.

Discipline Sounds Like This:

Les T., hospitality manager: "The turning point in my career was attending one of those time-management courses some years back. I was always disciplined, but the power grew when I learned how to use that discipline in an organized process every day. This little Palm Pilot means that I call my mom every Sunday rather than letting months go by without calling. It means I take my wife out for dinner every week without her asking. It means that my employees know that if I say I need to see something on Monday, I will be calling on Monday if I haven't seen it. This Palm Pilot is so much a part of my life that I have lengthened all of my pants pockets so that it fits right there on my hip."

Troy T., sales executive: "My filing system may not look that pretty, but it is very efficient. I write everything by hand because I know that no customer is going to see these files, so why waste time making them look pretty? My whole life as a salesperson is based on deadlines and follow-up. In my system, I keep track of everything so that I take responsibility not only for my deadlines and follow-up but for all of my customers' and colleagues' as well. If they haven't gotten back to me by the time they promised, they're going to receive an email from me. In fact, I heard from one the other day who said, 'I may as well get back to you because I know you're going to call me if you haven't heard from me.'"

Diedre S., office manager: "I hate wasting time, so I make lists — long lists that keep me on track. Today my list has ninety items on it, and I will get through ninety-five percent of them. And that's discipline because I don't let anybody waste my time. I am not rude, but I can let you know in a very tactful, humorous way that your time is up."

Ideas for Action

❏ Don't hesitate to check as often as necessary to ensure that things are right. You feel an urge to do it anyway, and soon others will come to expect it from you.

- Accept that mistakes might depress you. Precision is a core part of who you are; however, you must find ways to move through these moments of annoyance to prevent becoming discouraged.

- Recognize that others may not be as disciplined as you are. More than likely, their clumsy process will frustrate you, so try to look beyond it, and focus on their results, not on their process.

- Exactitude is your forte; you enjoy poring over details. Seek opportunities to peruse contracts, important communications or financial documents for errors. You can save yourself and others from making costly mistakes and looking foolish.

- Increasing efficiency is one of your hallmarks. You are a perfectionist at heart. Discover situations in which time or money is being wasted because of inefficiency, and create systems or procedures to improve efficiency.

- You not only create order, you probably also crave it in the form of a well-organized space. To completely free your Discipline talents, invest in furniture and organization systems that enable you to have "a place for everything and everything in its place."

- Timelines motivate you. When you have a task to complete, you like to know the deadline so you can plan your schedule accordingly. Apply your Discipline talents by outlining the step-by-step plan you will use. Others will appreciate your cues because they will help keep everyone "on task."

- ❏ Others may confuse your Discipline talents with rigidity. Help them understand that your discipline helps you pack more effectiveness into a day — often because you prioritize your time. When working with others who are not as disciplined, ask them to clarify deadlines so you can adjust your workload to accommodate their requests.

- ❏ Seek out roles and responsibilities that have structure.

- ❏ Create routines that require you to systematically follow through. Over time, people will come to appreciate this kind of predictability.

Working With Others Who Have Discipline

- ❏ When working on a project with people who have Discipline, make sure to give them advance notice of deadlines. They feel a need to get work done ahead of schedule, and they can't do this if you don't tell them the timelines.

- ❏ Try not to surprise people who have Discipline with sudden changes in plans and priorities. The unexpected is distressing to them. It can ruin their day.

- ❏ Disorganization will annoy people with Discipline. Don't expect them to last long in a physically cluttered environment.

EMPATHY

You can sense the emotions of those around you. You can feel what they are feeling as though their feelings are your own. Intuitively, you are able to see the world through their eyes and share their perspective. You do not necessarily agree with each person's perspective. You do not necessarily feel pity for each person's predicament — this would be sympathy, not Empathy. You do not necessarily condone the choices each person makes, but you do understand. This instinctive ability to understand is powerful. You hear the unvoiced questions. You anticipate the need. Where others grapple for words, you seem to find the right words and the right tone. You help people find the right phrases to express their feelings — to themselves as well as to others. You help them give voice to their emotional life. For all these reasons other people are drawn to you.

Empathy Sounds Like This:

Alyce J., administrator: "Recently, I was in a meeting of trustees where one of the individuals was presenting a new idea that was critical to her and to the life of this group. When she was finished, no one heard her opinion, no one really heard her. It was a powerfully demoralizing moment for her. I could see it in her face, and she wasn't herself for a day or two afterward. I finally raised the issue with her and used words that helped describe how she was feeling. I said, 'Something's wrong,' and she started to talk. I said, 'I really understand. I know how important this was for you, and you don't seem like yourself,' and so on. And she finally gave words to what was going on inside her. She said, 'You're the only one who heard me and who has said one word to me about it.'"

Brian H., administrator: "When my team is making decisions, what I like to do is say, 'Okay, what will this person say about this? What will that person say about it?' In other words, put yourself in their position. Let's think about the arguments from their perspective so that we can all be more persuasive."

Janet P., schoolteacher: "I never played basketball because they didn't have it for women when I was a kid, but I believe I can tell at a basketball game when the momentum is changing, and I want to go to the coach and say, 'Get them revved up. You are losing them.' Empathy also works in large groups; you can feel the crowd."

Ideas for Action

- Help your friends and colleagues be more aware when one of your peers is having a difficult time. Remember, most people do not have your ability to pick up on sensitive situations.

- Act quickly and firmly when others behave in a way that is unhealthy for themselves or others. Understanding someone's emotional state does not mean that you must excuse this behavior. Be aware that when your empathy turns to sympathy, others might see you as a "bleeding heart."

- Partner with someone with strong Command or Activator talents. This person will help you take needed action, even though people's feelings might suffer as a result.

- Consider serving others as a confidante or mentor. Because trust is paramount to you, people are likely to feel comfortable approaching you with any need. Your discretion and desire to be genuinely helpful will be greatly valued.

- At times, your empathy for others may overwhelm you. Create some rituals that you can use at the end of your day to signal that work is over. This will help buffer your emotions and prevent burnout.

- Identify a friend who also has strong Empathy talents, and check your observations with them.

- Sensitive to the feelings of others, you readily gauge the emotional tone of a room. Use your talents to forge a bridge of understanding and mutual support. Your empathy will be especially important during trying times because it will demonstrate your concern, thereby building loyalty.

- Witnessing the happiness of others brings you pleasure. Consequently, you are likely to be attuned to opportunities to underscore others' successes and positively reinforce their achievements. At each opportunity, deliver a kind word of appreciation or recognition. In doing so, you are likely to make a profound and engaging impression.

- Because you are observant of how others are feeling, you are likely to intuit what is about to happen before it becomes common knowledge. Although your intuitions may at times seem nothing more than "hunches," take conscious note of them. They may turn out to be valuable assets.

Empathy

- Sometimes empathy does not require words at all. A kind gesture may be all someone needs to be reassured. Use your Empathy talents to comfort others nonverbally with a glance, a smile or a pat on the arm.

Working With Others Who Have Empathy

- Ask people with Empathy to help you understand how certain people in your organization are feeling. They are sensitive to the emotions of others.

- Before securing commitment to a particular course of action from people with Empathy, ask them how they feel and how other people feel about the issues involved. For them, emotions are as real as other more practical factors and must be weighed when making decisions.

- When employees or customers have difficulty understanding why an action is necessary, ask people with Empathy for help. They may be able to sense what others are missing.

FOCUS

"Where am I headed?" you ask yourself. You ask this question every day. Guided by this theme of Focus, you need a clear destination. Lacking one, your life and your work can quickly become frustrating. And so each year, each month and even each week you set goals. These goals then serve as your compass, helping you determine priorities and make the necessary corrections to get back on course. Your Focus is powerful because it forces you to filter; you instinctively evaluate whether or not a particular action will help you move toward your goal. Those that don't are ignored. In the end, then, your Focus forces you to be efficient. Naturally, the flip side of this is that it causes you to become impatient with delays, obstacles and even tangents, no matter how intriguing they appear to be. This makes you an extremely valuable team member. When others start to wander down other avenues, you bring them back to the main road. Your Focus reminds everyone that if something is not helping you move toward your destination, then it is not important. And if it is not important, then it is not worth your time. You keep everyone on point.

Focus Sounds Like This:

Nick H., computer executive: "It is very important to me to be efficient. I'm the sort of guy who plays a round of golf in two and a half hours. When I was at Electronic Data Systems, I worked out a set list of questions so that I could conduct a review of each division in fifteen minutes. The founder, Ross Perot, called me 'The Dentist' because I would schedule a whole day of these in-and-out, fifteen-minute meetings."

Brad F., sales executive: "I am always sorting priorities, trying to figure out the most efficient route toward the goal so that there is very little dead time, very little wasted motion. For example, I will get multiple calls from customers who need me to call the service department for them, and rather than taking each one of these calls as they come and interrupting the priorities of the day, I group them together into one call at the end of the day and get it done."

Mike L., administrator: "People are amazed how I put things into perspective and stay on track. When people around the district are stuck on issues and caught on contrived barriers, I am able to pole-vault over them, re-establish the focus and keep things moving."

Doriane L., homemaker: "I am just the kind of person who likes to get to the point — in conversations, at work and even when I am shopping with my husband. He likes to try on lots of things and has a good time doing it, whereas I try one thing on, and if I like it and it is not horribly priced, I buy it. I'm a surgical shopper."

Ideas for Action

- ❑ When you set goals, discipline yourself to include timelines and measurements. They will provide regular proof that you are indeed making progress.

- ❑ Seek roles in which you can function independently. With your dominant Focus talents, you will be able to stay on track with little supervision.

- Your greatest worth as a team member might be helping others set goals. At the end of meetings, take responsibility for summarizing what was decided, for defining when these decisions will be acted on and for setting a date when the group will reconvene.

- Others will think, act and talk less efficiently than you do. Pay attention. Sometimes their "detours" will lead to discoveries and delights.

- Stretch your goal setting beyond work. If you find yourself becoming too focused on work goals, set goals for your personal life. They will give weight to your personal priorities and thereby help create balance in your life.

- Hours can disappear when you are intent on a task; you lose track of time. Make sure that all of your objectives are met and all of your priorities are followed by scheduling your efforts and sticking to that schedule.

Focus

- You function best when you can concentrate on a few well-defined initiatives and demands. Give yourself permission to reject projects or tasks that do not align with your overall mission. This will help you concentrate your efforts on your most important priorities — and will help others appreciate your need for focus.

- Take the time to write down your aspirations, and refer to them often. You will feel more in control of your life.

- At work, be sure to tell your manager your mid-term and short-term goals. This might well give your manager the confidence to give you the room you need.

- Make sure that the focus points you set for yourself take into consideration both quantity and quality. The integrity of your objectives will ensure that the application of your Focus talents leads to solid and long-lasting success.

Working With Others Who Have Focus

- When there are projects with critical deadlines, try to involve people with Focus. They instinctively honor timelines and commitments. As soon as they own a project with a deadline, they will concentrate all their energies on it until it's completed.

- Be aware that unstructured meetings will bother people with Focus. So when they are present at a meeting, try to follow the agenda.

- Don't expect people with Focus to always be sensitive to the feelings of others because getting their work done often takes priority over people's sensitivities.

FUTURISTIC

"Wouldn't it be great if ..." You are the kind of person who loves to peer over the horizon. The future fascinates you. As if it were projected on the wall, you see in detail what the future might hold, and this detailed picture keeps pulling you forward, into tomorrow. While the exact content of the picture will depend on your other strengths and interests — a better product, a better team, a better life or a better world — it will always be inspirational to you. You are a dreamer who sees visions of what could be and who cherishes those visions. When the present proves too frustrating and the people around you too pragmatic, you conjure up your visions of the future and they energize you. They can energize others too. In fact, very often people look to you to describe your visions of the future. They want a picture that can raise their sights and thereby their spirits. You can paint it for them. Practice. Choose your words carefully. Make the picture as vivid as possible. People will want to latch on to the hope you bring.

Futuristic Sounds Like This:

Dan F., school administrator: "In any situation, I am the guy who says, 'Did you ever think about ...? I wonder if we could ... I don't believe it can't be done. It's just that nobody has done it yet. Let's figure out how we can.' I am always looking for options, for ways not to be mired by the status quo. In fact, there is no such thing as the status quo. You are either moving forward, or you are moving backward. That's the reality of life, at least from my perspective. And right now, I believe that my profession is moving backward. State schools are being out-serviced by private schools, charter schools, home schools, internet schools. We need to free ourselves from our traditions and create a new future."

Jan K., internist: "Here at the Mayo Clinic, we are launching a group called the Hospitalists. Rather than having patients handed off from one doctor to another during their stay in the hospital, I envision a family of providers. I envision fifteen to twenty MDs, of various genders and races, with twenty to twenty-five nurse practitioners. There will be four to five new hospital services, most of which will work with surgeons and will provide para-operative care as well as care for the hospitalized elderly. We are redefining the model of care here. We don't just take care of the patients when they are in the hospital. If a patient comes in for a knee replacement, a member of the Hospitalist team would see them before the surgery, follow them from the day of surgery through the days of hospitalization and then see them when they come in six weeks later for their postoperative check. We will provide patients with a complete episode of care so that they don't get lost in the handoffs. And to get the funding, I just saw the detailed picture in my head and kept describing this picture to the department chair. I guess I made it seem so real that they had no choice but to grant me the funds."

Ideas for Action

❑ Choose roles in which you can contribute your ideas about the future. For example, you might excel in entrepreneurial or start-up situations.

❑ Take time to think about the future. The more time you spend considering your ideas about the future, the more vivid your ideas will become. The more vivid your ideas, the more persuasive you will be.

- ❑ Seek audiences that appreciate your ideas for the future. They will expect you to make these ideas a reality, and these expectations will motivate you.

- ❑ Find a friend or colleague who also has powerful Futuristic talents. Set aside an hour each month for "future" discussions. You can push each other to greater heights of creativity and vividness.

- ❑ Partner with someone with strong Activator talents. This person can remind you that you do not discover the future, you create it with the actions you take today.

- ❑ You inspire others with your images of the future, yet your thinking may be too expansive for them to comprehend. When you articulate your vision, be sure to describe the future in detail with vivid words and metaphors. Make your ideas and strategies more concrete via sketches, step-by-step action plans or mock-up models so that others can readily grasp your intent.

- ❑ Surround yourself with people who are eager to put your vision into motion. They will feel exhilarated by your Futuristic talents, and you can harness their energy to propel the vision toward reality.

- ❑ Be prepared to provide logical support for your futuristic thinking. Your exciting visions of future success will be best received when rooted in real possibility.

- ❑ Your Futuristic talents could equip you to be a guide or coach for others. Unlike you, they might not be able to easily see over the horizon. If you catch a vision of what someone could be or do, don't assume that they are aware of that potential. Share what you see as vividly as you can. In doing so, you may inspire someone to move forward.

- ❑ Musing about the future comes naturally to you. Read articles about technology, science and research to gain knowledge that will fuel your imagination.

Working With Others Who Have Futuristic

- ❑ Keep in mind that people with Futuristic live for the future. Ask them to share their vision with you — their vision about their career, about your organization, and about the marketplace or field in general.

- ❑ Stimulate people who have Futuristic by talking with them often about what could be. Ask lots of questions. Push them to make the future they see as vivid as possible.

- ❑ Send people with Futuristic any data or articles you spot that would be of interest to them. They need grist for their futuristic mill.

HARMONY

You look for areas of agreement. In your view there is little to be gained from conflict and friction, so you seek to hold them to a minimum. When you know that the people around you hold differing views, you try to find the common ground. You try to steer them away from confrontation and toward harmony. In fact, harmony is one of your guiding values. You can't quite believe how much time is wasted by people trying to impose their views on others. Wouldn't we all be more productive if we kept our opinions in check and instead looked for consensus and support? You believe we would, and you live by that belief. When others are sounding off about their goals, their claims and their fervently held opinions, you hold your peace. When others strike out in a direction, you will willingly, in the service of harmony, modify your own objectives to merge with theirs (as long as their basic values do not clash with yours). When others start to argue about their pet theory or concept, you steer clear of the debate, preferring to talk about practical, down-to-earth matters on which you can all agree. In your view we are all in the same boat, and we need this boat to get where we are going. It is a good boat. There is no need to rock it just to show that you can.

Harmony Sounds Like This:

Jane C., Benedictine nun: "I like people. I relate to them easily because I am very strong in adjustment. I take the shape of the vessel into which I am poured, so I don't irritate easily."

Chuck M., teacher: "I don't like conflict in class, but I have learned to let things run their course instead of trying to stop it right away. When I first started teaching, if someone said something negative, I would think, 'Oh, why did you have to say that?' and try to get rid of it right away. But now I simply try to get the opinion of someone else in the class so that perhaps we can have different points of view on the same topic."

Tom P., technician: "I can remember vividly when I was ten or eleven and some of the kids in my school would get into arguments. For some reason, I would feel compelled to get in the middle of things and find the common ground. I was the peacemaker."

Ideas for Action

❑ Use your Harmony talents to build a network of people with differing perspectives. Rely on these people when you need expertise. Your openness to these differing perspectives will help you learn.

❑ When two people are arguing, ask others in the group to share their thoughts. By increasing the number of voices in the conversation, you are more likely to find areas where all parties can agree. You can draw people together.

❑ Avoid roles that will lead you to confront people on a daily basis. Sales roles based on cold calls or roles in highly competitive workplaces, for example, will frustrate or upset you.

❑ Practice your techniques for resolving conflict without confrontation. Without these polished techniques, you might find yourself simply running away from conflicts, leaving them unresolved. This could lead you to passive-aggressive behavior.

- ❏ Partner with someone especially talented in Command or Activator. When all your best efforts to resolve a conflict have met with no success, this person can help you confront it head-on.

- ❏ Create interactions and forums in which people feel like their opinions are truly being heard. In doing so, you will help others become more engaged in group projects and activities.

- ❏ Be aware that your attempts to create harmony by allowing everyone a turn to speak might actually create disharmony in some people. Individuals with exceptional Achiever talents, for example, may be anxious to make a decision and take action. Learn to briefly yet effectively communicate the value of listening.

- ❏ Understand that some may take advantage of your efforts to produce harmony. On occasion, when everyone is getting an opportunity to speak, some individuals might waste time positioning themselves or getting into lofty debates that have little relevance to the task at hand. At these times, do not hesitate to jump in and turn the conversation around to more practical matters. A balance between listening and efficiency is key to harmony.

- ❏ In discussions, look for the practical side of things. Help others see this practical side. It is the starting point of agreement.

- ❏ Deference comes naturally for you. You easily step aside when someone with superior expertise enters. Take the next step by inviting those with greater expertise to consult.

Working With Others Who Have Harmony

- Steer people with Harmony as far as possible away from conflict. Try not to invite them to meetings where there will almost certainly be arguments, because they are not at their best when confronting others.

- Don't waste your time discussing controversial subjects with people who have Harmony. They will not enjoy debate for its own sake. Instead, keep your discussions focused on practical matters about which clear action can be taken.

- When others are locked in disagreement, people with Harmony can help unlock them. They will not necessarily resolve the subject under debate, but they will help people find other areas where they agree. This common ground can be the starting point for working productively together.

IDEATION

You are fascinated by ideas. What is an idea? An idea is a concept, the best explanation of the most events. You are delighted when you discover beneath the complex surface an elegantly simple concept to explain why things are the way they are. An idea is a connection. Yours is the kind of mind that is always looking for connections, and so you are intrigued when seemingly disparate phenomena can be linked by an obscure connection. An idea is a new perspective on familiar challenges. You revel in taking the world we all know and turning it around so we can view it from a strange but strangely enlightening angle. You love all these ideas because they are profound, because they are novel, because they are clarifying, because they are contrary, because they are bizarre. For all these reasons you derive a jolt of energy whenever a new idea occurs to you. Others may label you creative or original or conceptual or even smart. Perhaps you are all of these. Who can be sure? What you are sure of is that ideas are thrilling. And on most days this is enough.

Ideation Sounds Like This:

Mark B., writer: "My mind works by finding connections between things. When I was hunting down the Mona Lisa in the Louvre museum, I turned a corner and was blinded by the flashing of a thousand cameras snapping the tiny picture. For some reason, I stored that visual image away. Then I noticed a 'No Flash Photography' sign, and I stored that away too. I thought it was odd because I remembered reading that flash photography can harm paintings. Then about six months later, I read that the Mona Lisa has been stolen at least twice in this century. And suddenly I put it all together. The only explanation for all these facts is that the real Mona Lisa is not on display in the Louvre. The real Mona Lisa has been stolen, and the museum, afraid to admit their carelessness, has installed a fake. I don't know if it's true, of course, but what a great story."

Andrea H., interior designer: "I have the kind of mind where everything has to fit together or I start to feel very odd. For me, every piece of furniture represents an idea. It serves a discrete function both independently and in concert with every other piece. The 'idea' of each piece is so powerful in my mind, it must be obeyed. If I am sitting in a room where the chairs are somehow not fulfilling their discrete function — they're the wrong kind of chairs or they're facing the wrong way or they're pushed up too close to the coffee table — I find myself getting physically uncomfortable and mentally distracted. Later, I won't be able to get it out of my mind. I'll find myself awake at 3:00 a.m., and I walk through the person's house in my mind's eye, rearranging the furniture and repainting the walls. This started happening when I was very young, say seven years old."

Ideas for Action

- ❑ Seek a career in which you will be given credit for and paid for your ideas, such as marketing, advertising, journalism, design or new product development.

- ❑ You are likely to get bored quickly, so make some small changes in your work or home life. Experiment. Play mental games with yourself. All of these will help keep you stimulated.

- Finish your thoughts and ideas before communicating them. Lacking your Ideation talents, others might not be able to "join the dots" of an interesting but incomplete idea and thus might dismiss it.

- Not all your ideas will be equally practical or serviceable. Learn to edit your ideas, or find a trusted friend or colleague who can "proof" your ideas and identify potential pitfalls.

- Understand the fuel for your Ideation talents: When do you get your best ideas? When you're talking with people? When you're reading? When you're simply listening or observing? Take note of the circumstances that seem to produce your best ideas, and recreate them.

- Schedule time to read, because the ideas and experiences of others can become your raw material for new ideas. Schedule time to think, because thinking energizes you.

- You are a natural fit with research and development; you appreciate the mindset of visionaries and dreamers. Spend time with imaginative peers, and sit in on their brainstorming sessions.

- Partner with someone with strong Analytical talents. This person will question you and challenge you, therefore strengthening your ideas.

- Sometimes you lose others' interest because they cannot follow your abstract and conceptual thinking style. Make your ideas more concrete by drawing pictures, using analogies or metaphors, or simply explaining your concepts step by step.

- Feed your Ideation talents by gathering knowledge. Study fields and industries that are different from your own. Apply ideas from outside, and link disparate ideas to generate new ones.

Working With Others Who Have Ideation

- People with Ideation enjoy the power of words. Whenever you come across a word combination that perfectly captures a concept, idea or pattern, share it with them. It will stimulate their thinking.

- People who have Ideation will be particularly effective as designers, whether of sales strategies, marketing campaigns, customer service solutions or new products. Whenever possible, try to make the most of their ability to create.

- Try to feed people who have Ideation new ideas; they thrive on them. They will not only be more excited about their work, but they will also use these new concepts to generate new insights and discoveries of their own.

INCLUDER

"Stretch the circle wider." This is the philosophy around which you orient your life. You want to include people and make them feel part of the group. In direct contrast to those who are drawn only to exclusive groups, you actively avoid those groups that exclude others. You want to expand the group so that as many people as possible can benefit from its support. You hate the sight of someone on the outside looking in. You want to draw them in so that they can feel the warmth of the group. You are an instinctively accepting person. Regardless of race or sex or nationality or personality or faith, you cast few judgments. Judgments can hurt a person's feelings. Why do that if you don't have to? Your accepting nature does not necessarily rest on a belief that each of us is different and that one should respect these differences. Rather, it rests on your conviction that fundamentally we are all the same. We are all equally important. Thus, no one should be ignored. Each of us should be included. It is the least we all deserve.

Includer Sounds Like This:

Harry B., outplacement consultant: "Even as a child, although I was very shy, I always made sure that I was the one inviting others to play. When picking teams or sides in school, I never wanted anyone not to participate with us. In fact, I can remember when I was ten or eleven, I had a friend who was not a member of our church. We were at a church banquet, and he showed up at the door because typically we had our youth activity at the church on that night. Immediately, I got up, brought him over to our family and sat him down at the table."

Jeremy B., defense lawyer: "When I first started this job, I met people and became fast, furious friends with them almost on day one, only to find out later that, you know, this person's got a lot of issues, and I've already included them in dinner parties and our social circle. My partner, Mark, is like, 'What is it exactly that made you want to include this person?' And then it's a matter of figuring out what pushed my buttons when I first met them, what made me enjoy them so much. And, you know, making sure that this is the aspect of them that Mark and I focus on ... because once I include someone in my circle, I don't dump them."

Giles D., corporate trainer: "In class, I seem to be able to sense when someone is disengaging from the group discussion, and I immediately draw them back into the conversation. Last week, we got into a lengthy discussion about performance appraisals, and one woman wasn't talking at all. So I just said, 'Monica, you've had performance appraisals. Any thoughts on the subject?' I really think this has helped me as a teacher because when I don't know the answer to something, very often it is the person I pull in who supplies the answer for me."

Ideas for Action

❏ Consider roles in which you can take responsibility for representing voices that are not usually heard. You will derive a great deal of satisfaction from being a spokesperson for these people.

❏ Look for opportunities to bring together people of diverse cultures and backgrounds. You can be a leader in this area.

- ❏ Help those who are new to an organization or group get to know other people. You will always be adept at quickly making people feel accepted and involved.

- ❏ An anti-elitist, you may clash with those who feel they have earned the right to perks and power. Rather than disputing their claim, use your Includer insights to help everyone find common ground and value in their contributions.

- ❏ Acknowledge the dissonance you feel when you must be the bearer of bad news. Look for partners who can help you justify your position so you don't apologize or soften the message too much.

- ❏ Not every person is lovable or even likeable. While many of your friends or colleagues may be put off by difficult people, you have a natural capacity to truly care for all people. Let others know that if they ever come to the end of their rope with a problematic individual, they can call on you to step in.

- ❏ Choose roles in which you are continuously working and interacting with people. You will enjoy the challenge of making everyone feel important.

- ❏ Partner with someone who has dominant Activator or Command talents. This person can help you when you have to deliver news that might hurt someone's feelings.

- ❏ Realize that people will relate to each other through you. You are a conduit for information. You can interact with all parts and all people in a group and keep them effectively connected to each other.

- Explain what we all have in common. Help others understand that to respect the differences among us (our diversity), we must begin by appreciating what we all share (our similarity).

Working With Others Who Have Includer

- When you have group functions, ask people with Includer to help ensure that everyone is included. They will work hard to see that no individual or group is overlooked.

- Ask people with Includer to help you think about potential customers, markets or opportunities you are not reaching today.

- If you are not a "natural" in social settings, stay close to people who have Includer. They will make sure you are a part of the conversation.

INDIVIDUALIZATION

Your Individualization theme leads you to be intrigued by the unique qualities of each person. You are impatient with generalizations or "types" because you don't want to obscure what is special and distinct about each person. Instead, you focus on the differences between individuals. You instinctively observe each person's style, each person's motivation, how each thinks and how each builds relationships. You hear the one-of-a-kind stories in each person's life. This theme explains why you pick your friends just the right birthday gift, why you know that one person prefers praise in public and another detests it, and why you tailor your teaching style to accommodate one person's need to be shown and another's desire to "figure it out as I go." Because you are such a keen observer of other people's strengths, you can draw out the best in each person. This Individualization theme also helps you build productive teams. While some search around for the perfect team "structure" or "process," you know instinctively that the secret to great teams is casting by individual strengths so that everyone can do a lot of what they do well.

Individualization Sounds Like This:

Les T., hospitality manager: "Carl is one of our best performers, but he still has to see me every week. He just wants a little encouragement and to check in, and he gets fired up a little bit after that meeting. Greg doesn't like to meet very often, so there's no need for me to bother him. And when we do meet, it's really for me, not for him."

Marsha D., publishing executive: "Sometimes I would walk out of my office and — you know how cartoon characters have those balloons over their head? I would see these little balloons over everyone's head telling me what was in their minds. It sounds weird, doesn't it? But it happens all the time."

Andrea H., interior designer: "When you ask people what their style is, they find it hard to describe, so I just ask them, 'What is your favorite spot in the house?' And when I ask that, their faces light up, and they know just where to take me. From that one spot, I can begin to piece together the kind of people they are and what their style is."

Ideas for Action

- ❏ Select a vocation in which your Individualization talents can be both used and appreciated, such as counseling, supervising, teaching, writing human interest articles or selling. Your ability to see people as unique individuals is a special talent.

- ❏ Become an expert in describing your own strengths and style. For example, answer questions such as: What is the best praise you ever received? How often do you like to check in with your manager? What is your best method for building relationships? How do you learn best? Then ask your colleagues and friends these same questions. Help them plan their future by starting with their strengths, then designing a future based on what they do best.

- ❏ Help others understand that true diversity can be found in the subtle differences between each individual — regardless of race, sex or nationality.

- Explain that it is appropriate, just and effective to treat each person differently. Those without strong Individualization talents might not see the differences among individuals and might insist that individualization is unequal and therefore unfair. You will need to describe your perspective in detail to be persuasive.

- Figure out what every person on your team does best. Then help them capitalize on their talents, skills and knowledge. You may need to explain your rationale and your philosophy so people understand that you have their best interests in mind.

- You have an awareness and appreciation of others' likes and dislikes and an ability to personalize. This puts you in a unique position. Use your Individualization talents to help identify areas where one size does not fit all.

- Make your colleagues and friends aware of each person's unique needs. Soon people will look to you to explain other people's motivations and actions.

- Your presentations and speaking opportunities will be most engaging when you relate your topic to the experiences of individuals in the audience. Use your Individualization talents to gather and share real-life stories that will make your points much better than generic information or theories would.

- You move comfortably among a broad range of styles and cultures, and you intuitively personalize your interactions. Consciously and proactively make full use of these talents by leading diversity and community efforts.

Individualization

- Your Individualization talents can help you take a different approach to interpreting data. While others are looking for similarities, make a point of identifying distinctiveness. Your interpretations will add a valuable perspective.

Working With Others Who Have Individualization

- When you are having difficulty understanding someone else's perspective, turn to people with Individualization for insight. They can show you the world through others' eyes.

- If you want to learn more about your unique talents and how you stand out in a crowd, ask people with Individualization for their insights.

- Have a discussion with people who have Individualization when you are having problems with a coworker. Their intuitions about the appropriate action for each individual will be sound.

INPUT

You are inquisitive. You collect things. You might collect information — words, facts, books and quotations — or you might collect tangible objects such as butterflies, baseball cards, porcelain dolls or sepia photographs. Whatever you collect, you collect it because it interests you. And yours is the kind of mind that finds so many things interesting. The world is exciting precisely because of its infinite variety and complexity. If you read a great deal, it is not necessarily to refine your theories but, rather, to add more information to your archives. If you like to travel, it is because each new location offers novel artifacts and facts. These can be acquired and then stored away. Why are they worth storing? At the time of storing it is often hard to say exactly when or why you might need them, but who knows when they might become useful? With all those possible uses in mind, you really don't feel comfortable throwing anything away. So you keep acquiring and compiling and filing stuff away. It's interesting. It keeps your mind fresh. And perhaps one day some of it will prove valuable.

Input Sounds Like This:

Ellen K., writer: "Even as a child, I found myself wanting to know everything. I would make a game of my questions. 'What is my question today?' I would think up these outrageous questions, and then I would go looking for the books that would answer them. I often got in way over my head, deep into books that I didn't have a clue about, but I read them because they had my answer someplace. My questions became my tool for leading me from one piece of information to another."

John F., human resources executive: "I'm one of those people who thinks that the internet is the greatest thing since sliced bread. I used to feel so frustrated, but now if I want to know what the stock market is doing in a certain area or the rules of a certain game or what the GNP of Spain is or other different things, I just go to the computer, start looking and eventually find it."

Kevin F., salesperson: "I'm amazed at some of the garbage that collects in my mind, and I love playing *Jeopardy* and Trivial Pursuit and anything like that. I don't mind throwing things away as long as they're material things, but I hate wasting knowledge or accumulated knowledge or not being able to read something fully if I enjoy it."

Ideas for Action

- Look for jobs in which you are charged with acquiring new information each day, such as teaching, research or journalism.

- Devise a system to store and easily locate information. This can be as simple as a file for all the articles you have clipped or as sophisticated as a computer database.

- Partner with someone with dominant Focus or Discipline talents. This person will help you stay on track when your inquisitiveness leads you down intriguing but distracting avenues.

- Your mind is open and absorbent. You naturally soak up information in the same way that a sponge soaks up water. But just as the primary purpose of the sponge is not to permanently contain what it absorbs, neither should your mind simply store information. Input without output can lead to stagnation. As you gather and absorb information, be aware of the individuals and groups that can most benefit from your knowledge, and be intentional about sharing with them.

- You might naturally be an exceptional repository of facts, data and ideas. If that's the case, don't be afraid to position yourself as an expert. By simply following your Input talents, you could become known as the authority in your field.

- Remember that you must be more than just a collector of information. At some point, you'll need to leverage this knowledge and turn it into action. Make a point of identifying the facts and data that would be most valuable to others, and use this information to their advantage.

- Identify your areas of specialization, and actively seek more information about them.

- Schedule time to read books and articles that stimulate you.

- Deliberately increase your vocabulary. Collect new words, and learn the meaning of each of them.

- Identify situations in which you can share the information you have collected with other people. Also make sure to let your friends and colleagues know that you enjoy answering their questions.

Working With Others Who Have Input

- ❏ Keep people with Input posted on the latest news. They need to be in the know. Pass along books, articles and papers you think they would like to read.

- ❏ See if you can find a few common interests with people who have Input, and then share facts and stories on these topics. This is often how great relationships begin.

- ❏ When you are in meetings, make a point of asking people with Input for information. Look for opportunities to leverage their abundant knowledge.

INTELLECTION

You like to think. You like mental activity. You like exercising the "muscles" of your brain, stretching them in multiple directions. This need for mental activity may be focused; for example, you may be trying to solve a problem or develop an idea or understand another person's feelings. The exact focus will depend on your other strengths. On the other hand, this mental activity may very well lack focus. The theme of Intellection does not dictate what you are thinking about; it simply describes that you like to think. You are the kind of person who enjoys your time alone because it is your time for musing and reflection. You are introspective. In a sense you are your own best companion, as you pose yourself questions and try out answers on yourself to see how they sound. This introspection may lead you to a slight sense of discontent as you compare what you are actually doing with all the thoughts and ideas that your mind conceives. Or this introspection may tend toward more pragmatic matters such as the events of the day or a conversation that you plan to have later. Wherever it leads you, this mental hum is one of the constants of your life.

Intellection Sounds Like This:

Lauren H., project manager: "I suppose that most people who meet me in passing presume that I am a flaming extrovert. I do not deny the fact that I love people, but they would be amazed to know how much time alone, how much solitude, I need in order to function in public. I really love my own company. I love solitude because it gives me a chance to allow my diffused focus to simmer with something else. That's where my best ideas come from. My ideas need to simmer and 'perk.' I used this phrase even when I was younger: 'I have put my ideas in, and now I have to wait for them to perk.'"

Michael P., marketing executive: "It's strange, but I find that I need to have noise around me or I can't concentrate. I need to have parts of my brain occupied; otherwise, it goes so fast in so many directions that I don't get anything done. If I can occupy my brain with the TV or my kids running around, then I find I concentrate even better."

Jorge H., factory manager and former political prisoner: "We used to get put into solitary confinement as a punishment, but I never hated it as much as the others did. You might think that you would get lonely, but I never did. I used the time to reflect on my life and sort out the kind of man I was and what was really important to me: my family, my values. In a weird way, solitary actually calmed me down and made me stronger."

Ideas for Action

- Consider beginning or continuing your studies in philosophy, literature or psychology. You will always enjoy subjects that stimulate your thinking.

- List your ideas in a log or diary. These ideas will serve as grist for your mental mill, and they might yield valuable insights.

- Deliberately build relationships with people you consider to be "big thinkers." Their example will inspire you to focus your own thinking.

- People may think you are aloof or disengaged when you close your door or spend time alone. Help them understand that this is simply a reflection of your thinking style and that it results not from a disregard for relationships, but from a desire to bring the most you can to those relationships.

❑ You are at your best when you have the time to follow an intellectual trail and see where it leads. Get involved on the front end of projects and initiatives, rather than jumping in at the execution stage. If you join in the latter stages, you may derail what has already been decided, and your insights may come too late.

❑ Engaging people in intellectual and philosophical debate is one way that you make sense of things. This is not the case for everyone. Be sure to channel your provocative questions to those who similarly enjoy the give and take of debate.

❑ Schedule time for thinking; it can be energizing for you. Use these occasions to muse and reflect.

❑ Take time to write. Writing might be the best way for you to crystallize and integrate your thoughts.

❑ Find people who like to talk about the same issues you do. Organize a discussion group that addresses your subjects of interest.

Intellection

❑ Encourage people around you to use their full intellectual capital by reframing questions for them and by engaging them in dialogue. At the same time, realize that there will be some who find this intimidating and who need time to reflect before being put on the spot.

Working With Others Who Have Intellection

- ❑ When working with people who have Intellection, don't hesitate to challenge their thinking; they probably won't be threatened by it. On the contrary, they should take it as a sign that you're paying attention to them.

- ❑ When you're faced with books, articles or proposals that need to be evaluated, ask people with Intellection to read them and let you know what they think. They love to read.

- ❑ Capitalize on the fact that thinking energizes people with Intellection. For example, when you need to explain why something has to be done, ask them to think it through and to help you uncover a detailed explanation.

LEARNER

You love to learn. The subject matter that interests you most will be determined by your other themes and experiences, but whatever the subject, you will always be drawn to the process of learning. The process, more than the content or the result, is especially exciting for you. You are energized by the steady and deliberate journey from ignorance to competence. The thrill of the first few facts, the early efforts to recite or practice what you have learned, the growing confidence of a skill mastered — this is the process that entices you. Your excitement leads you to engage in adult learning experiences — yoga or piano lessons or graduate classes. It enables you to thrive in dynamic work environments where you are asked to take on short project assignments and are expected to learn a lot about the new subject matter in a short period of time and then move on to the next one. This Learner theme does not necessarily mean that you seek to become the subject matter expert, or that you are striving for the respect that accompanies a professional or academic credential. The outcome of the learning is less significant than the "getting there."

Learner Sounds Like This:

Annie M., managing editor: "I get antsy when I am not learning something. Last year, although I was enjoying my work, I didn't feel as though I was learning enough. So I took up tap dancing. It sounds strange, doesn't it? I know I am never going to perform or anything, but I enjoy focusing on the technical skill of tapping, getting a little better each week and moving up from the beginners' class to the intermediate class. That was a kick."

Miles A., operations manager: "When I was seven years old, my teachers would tell my parents, 'Miles isn't the most intelligent boy in the school, but he's a sponge for learning, and he'll probably go really far because he will push himself and continually be grasping new things.' Right now, I am just starting a course in business-travel Spanish. I know it is probably too ambitious to think I could learn conversational Spanish and become totally proficient in that language, but I at least want to be able to travel there and know the language."

Tim S., coach for executives: "One of my clients is so inquisitive that it drives him crazy because he can't do everything he wants to. I'm different. I am not curious in that broad sense. I prefer to go into greater depth with things so that I can become competent in them and then use them at work. For example, recently one of my clients wanted me to travel with him to Nice, France, for a business engagement. So I started reading up on the region, buying books and checking the internet. It was all interesting and I enjoyed the study, but I wouldn't have done any of it if I wasn't going to be traveling there for work."

Ideas for Action

- ❑ Refine how you learn. For example, you might learn best by teaching; if so, seek out opportunities to present to others. You might learn best through quiet reflection; if so, find this quiet time.

- ❑ Develop ways to track the progress of your learning. If there are distinct levels or stages of learning within a discipline or skill, take a moment to celebrate your progression from one level to the next. If no such levels exist, create them for yourself (e.g., reading five books on the subject or making three presentations on the subject).

- ❑ Be a catalyst for change. Others might be intimidated by new rules, new skills or new circumstances. Your willingness to soak up this newness can calm their fears and spur them to action. Take this responsibility seriously.

- ❑ Seek roles that require some form of technical competence. You will enjoy the process of acquiring and maintaining this expertise.

- ❑ As far as possible, shift your career toward a field with constantly changing technologies or regulations. You will be energized by the challenge of keeping up.

- ❑ Because you are not threatened by unfamiliar information, you might excel in a consulting role (either internal or external) in which you are paid to go into new situations and pick up new competencies or languages quickly.

- ❑ Research supports the link between learning and performance. When people have the opportunity to learn and grow, they are more productive and loyal. Look for ways to measure the degree to which you and others feel that your learning needs are being met, to create individualized learning milestones and to reward achievements in learning.

- ❑ At work, take advantage of programs that subsidize your learning. Your organization may be willing to pay for part or all of your instructional coursework or for certifications. Ask your manager for information about scholarships and other educational opportunities.

- ❏ Honor your desire to learn. Take advantage of adult educational opportunities in your community. Discipline yourself to sign up for at least one new academic or adult learning course each year.

- ❏ Time disappears and your attention intensifies when you are immersed in studying or learning. Allow yourself to "follow the trail" by scheduling learning sessions during periods of time that will not be interrupted by pressing engagements.

Working With Others Who Have Learner

- ❏ Regardless of their role, people with Learner will be eager to learn new facts, skills or knowledge. Help them find new ways to learn and get motivated.

- ❏ Help people with Learner track their learning progress by identifying milestones or levels that they have reached. Celebrate these achievements.

- ❏ Encourage people who have Learner to become the "master" or "resident expert" in a specific area. This will feed their need for extreme competency.

MAXIMIZER

Excellence, not average, is your measure. Taking something from below average to slightly above average takes a great deal of effort and in your opinion is not very rewarding. Transforming something strong into something superb takes just as much effort but is much more thrilling. Strengths, whether yours or someone else's, fascinate you. Like a diver after pearls, you search them out, watching for the telltale signs of a strength. A glimpse of untutored excellence, rapid learning, a skill mastered without recourse to steps — all these are clues that a strength may be in play. And having found a strength, you feel compelled to nurture it, refine it and stretch it toward excellence. You polish the pearl until it shines. This natural sorting of strengths means that others see you as discriminating. You choose to spend time with people who appreciate your particular strengths. Likewise, you are attracted to others who seem to have found and cultivated their own strengths. You tend to avoid those who want to fix you and make you well-rounded. You don't want to spend your life bemoaning what you lack. Rather, you want to capitalize on the gifts with which you are blessed. It's more fun. It's more productive. And, counterintuitively, it is more demanding.

Maximizer Sounds Like This:

Gavin T., flight attendant: "I taught aerobics for ten years, and I made a point of asking people to focus on what they liked about themselves. We all have parts of our body that we would like to change or that we would like to see differently, but to focus on that can be so destructive. It becomes a vicious cycle. So I would say, 'Look, you don't need to be doing that. Instead, let's focus on the attribute you like about yourself, and then we'll all feel better about expending all of this energy.'"

Amy T., magazine editor: "There is nothing I hate more than having to fix a poorly written piece. If I have given the writer a clear focus and they come back with a piece that is completely off the mark, I almost can't bring myself to write comments on it. I'm more inclined to just hand it back to them and say, 'Just please start again.' On the other hand, what I love to do is take a piece that is so close and then refine it to make it perfect. You know, just the right word here, a little cut there, and suddenly it's a brilliant piece."

Marshall G., marketing executive: "I am really good at setting a focus for people and then building a sense of team spirit as we all march forward. But I am not so good at strategic thinking. Fortunately, I have a boss who understands that about me. We have been working together for quite a few years. He has found people who play the strategic role, and at the same time, stretches me to be even better at the focus and team-building role. I'm so lucky to have a boss who thinks this way. It's made me more secure and made me charge ahead much faster, knowing that my boss knows what I am good at and what I'm not good at; he doesn't bother me with the latter."

Ideas for Action

❑ Seek roles in which you are helping people succeed. In coaching, managing, mentoring or teaching roles, your focus on strengths will prove particularly beneficial to others. Because most people find it difficult to describe what they do best, start by arming them with vivid descriptions.

- Devise ways to measure your performance and the performance of others. These measures will help you spot strengths, because the best way to identify a strength is to look for sustained levels of excellent performance.

- Once you have identified your own greatest talents, stay focused on them. Refine your skills. Acquire new knowledge. Practice. Keep working toward strength in a few areas.

- Develop a plan to use your most powerful talents outside of work. In doing so, consider how your talents relate to the mission in your life and how they might benefit your family or the community.

- Problem solving might drain your energy and enthusiasm. Look for a restorative partner who can be your chief troubleshooter and problem solver. Let that person know how important your partnership is to your success.

- Study success. Deliberately spend time with people who have discovered their strengths. The more you understand how marshaling strengths leads to success, the more likely you will be to create success in your own life.

- Explain to others why you spend more time building on great talent rather than fixing weaknesses. Initially, they might confuse what you are doing with complacency.

- Don't let your Maximizer talents be stifled by conventional wisdom, which says you should find what is broken and fix it. Identify and invest in the parts of your organization or community that are working. Make sure that most of your resources are spent in the build-up and build-out of these pockets of excellence.

❑ Keep your focus on long-term relationships and goals. Many make a career out of picking the low-hanging fruit of short-term success, but your Maximizer talents will be most energized and effective as you turn top potential into true and lasting greatness.

❑ See if you can make some of your weaknesses irrelevant. For example, find a partner, devise a support system or use one of your stronger talents to compensate for one of your weaker ones.

Working With Others Who Have Maximizer

❑ People with Maximizer are interested in taking something that works and figuring out how to make the most of it. They may not be particularly interested in fixing things that are broken. If possible, avoid asking Maximizers to do things that demand continual problem solving. Instead, ask them for help when you need to uncover best practices.

❑ If you do not have someone around you who regularly focuses on your strengths, spend more time with people who have Maximizer. They are naturally inquisitive about excellence and will help you hone in on what you do best.

❑ People with Maximizer will expect you to understand and value their strengths. They will become frustrated if you spend too much time focusing on their weaknesses.

POSITIVITY

You are generous with praise, quick to smile and always on the lookout for the positive in the situation. Some call you lighthearted. Others just wish that their glass were as full as yours seems to be. But either way, people want to be around you. Their world looks better around you because your enthusiasm is contagious. Lacking your energy and optimism, some find their world drab with repetition or, worse, heavy with pressure. You seem to find a way to lighten their spirit. You inject drama into every project. You celebrate every achievement. You find ways to make everything more exciting and more vital. Some cynics may reject your energy, but you are rarely dragged down. Your Positivity won't allow it. Somehow you can't quite escape your conviction that it is good to be alive, that work can be fun and that no matter what the setbacks, one must never lose one's sense of humor.

Positivity Sounds Like This:

Gerry L., flight attendant: "There are so many people on an airplane that I have made it a point over the years to single out one or two on a flight and make it something special for them. Certainly, I will be courteous to everybody and extend to them the kind of professionalism that I would like given to me, but over and above that, I try to make one person or family or small group of people feel particularly special, with jokes and conversation and little games that I play."

Andy B., internet marketing executive: "I am one of those people who loves creating buzz. I read magazines all the time, and if I find something fun — some new store, new lip gloss, whatever — I will charge around telling everyone about it.

'Oh, you just have to try this store. It is so-o-o cool. Look at these pictures. Check them out.' I am so passionate when I talk about something that people just have to do what I say. It's not that I am a great salesperson. I'm not. In fact, I hate asking for the close; I hate bothering people. It's just that my passion about what I say makes people think, 'Gosh, it must be true.'"

Sunny G., communications manager: "I think the world is plagued with enough negative people. We need more positive people — people who like to zero in on what is right with the world. Negative people just make me feel heavy. In my last job, there was a guy who came into my office every morning just to unload on me. I would purposely dodge him. I'd see him coming, and I'd run to the bathroom or go some other place. He made me feel as if the world was a miserable place, and I hated that."

Ideas for Action

❏ You probably will excel in any role in which you are paid to highlight the positive. A teaching role, a sales role, an entrepreneurial role or a leadership role will make the most of your ability to make things dramatic.

❏ You tend to be more enthusiastic and energetic than most people. When others become discouraged or are reluctant to take risks, your attitude will provide the impetus to keep them moving. Over time, others will start to look to you for this "lift."

❏ Plan highlight activities for your friends and colleagues. For example, find ways to turn small achievements into events, plan regular celebrations that others can look forward to, or capitalize on the year's holidays and festivals.

- Explain that your enthusiasm is not simple naivety. You know that bad things can happen; you simply prefer to focus on the good things.

- You may get your greatest joy by encouraging people. Freely show your appreciation of others, and make sure that the praise is not vague. Consistently seek to translate your feelings into specific, tangible and personal expressions of gratitude and recognition.

- As you share your Positivity talents, be sure to protect and nurture them. As necessary, insulate yourself from chronic whiners and complainers, and intentionally spend time in highly positive environments that will invigorate and feed your optimism.

- Don't pretend that difficulties don't concern you. Other people need to know that while you find the good in virtually every situation, you are not naïve. Recognize challenges, and communicate the reasons for your optimism. Your positive approach will be most powerful when others realize it is grounded in reality.

- Because people will rely on you to help them rise above their daily frustrations, arm yourself with good stories, jokes and sayings. Never underestimate the effect that you can have on people.

- Avoid negative people. They will bring you down. Instead, seek people who find the same kind of drama and humor in the world that you do. You will energize each other.

- Deliberately help others see the things that are going well for them. You can keep their eyes on the positive.

Working With Others Who Have Positivity

- People with Positivity bring drama and energy to the workplace. They will make your organization more positive and dynamic.

- This theme doesn't imply that people who have Positivity are always in a good mood. But it does imply that through their humor and attitude, they can make people more excited about work. Remind them of this strength, and encourage them to use it.

- When working with people who have Positivity, be aware that cynics will quickly sap their energy. Don't expect them to enjoy cheering up negative people. They will do better when they can energize basically positive people who are simply in need of a spark.

RELATOR

Relator describes your attitude toward your relationships. In simple terms, the Relator theme pulls you toward people you already know. You do not necessarily shy away from meeting new people — in fact, you may have other themes that cause you to enjoy the thrill of turning strangers into friends — but you do derive a great deal of pleasure and strength from being around your close friends. You are comfortable with intimacy. Once the initial connection has been made, you deliberately encourage a deepening of the relationship. You want to understand their feelings, their goals, their fears and their dreams; and you want them to understand yours. You know that this kind of closeness implies a certain amount of risk — you might be taken advantage of — but you are willing to accept that risk. For you a relationship has value only if it is genuine. And the only way to know that is to entrust yourself to the other person. The more you share with each other, the more you risk together. The more you risk together, the more each of you proves your caring is genuine. These are your steps toward real friendship, and you take them willingly.

Relator Sounds Like This:

Jamie T., entrepreneur: "I'm definitely selective about my relationships. When I first meet people, I don't want to give them very much of my time. I don't know them; they don't know me — so let's just be pleasant and leave it at that. But if circumstances make it so that we get to know each other better, it seems like a threshold is reached where I suddenly start wanting to invest more. I'll share more of myself, put myself out for them, do things for them that will bring us a little closer and show that I care. It's funny because I am not looking for any more friends in my life. I have enough. And yet with each new person I meet, as soon as that threshold is reached, I feel compelled to go deeper and deeper. Now I have ten people working for me, and I would call each of them my very good friend."

Gavin T., flight attendant: "I have many wonderful acquaintances, but as for true friends that I hold dear, not very many. And I'm real okay with that. My best times are spent with the people I'm tightest with, like my family. We are a very tight-knit Irish Catholic family, and we get together every chance we can. It's a large family — I have five brothers and sisters and ten nieces and nephews — but we all get together about once a month and yuk it up. I'm the catalyst. When I'm back in Chicago, even if there is no birthday or anniversary or whatever, I become the excuse for getting together and hanging out for three or four days. We really enjoy one another's company."

Tony D., pilot: "I used to fly in the Marines, and, boy, you had better be comfortable with the word 'friend' in the Marines. You had better feel good about trusting someone else. I can't tell you how many times I put my life in someone else's hands. I was flying off my friend's wing, and I'd be dead if he couldn't get me back safely."

Ideas for Action

❏ Find a workplace in which friendships are encouraged. You will not do well in an overly formal organization. In job interviews, ask about work styles and company culture.

- ❏ Deliberately learn as much as you can about the people you meet. You like knowing about people, and other people like being known. By doing this, you will act as a catalyst for trusting relationships.

- ❏ Let it be known that you are more interested in the character and personality of others than in their status or job title. This is one of your greatest talents and can serve as a model for others.

- ❏ Let your caring show. For example, find people in your company to mentor, help your colleagues get to know each other better or extend your relationships beyond the office.

- ❏ No matter how busy you are, stay in contact with your friends. They are your fuel.

- ❏ Be honest with your friends. True caring means helping other people be successful and fulfilled. Giving honest feedback or encouraging your friends to move out of a role in which they are struggling is a compassionate act.

- ❏ You probably prefer to be seen as a person, an equal or a friend rather than as a function, a superior or a title. Let people know that they can address you by your first name rather than formally.

- ❏ You might tend to withhold the most engaging aspects of your personality until you have sensed openness from another person. Remember, building relationships is not a one-way street. Proactively "put yourself out there." Others will quickly see you for the genuine individual you are, and you will create many more opportunities to cultivate strong, long-lasting connections.

Relator

- ❏ Make time for family and close friends. You need to spend quality moments with those you love in order to "feed" your Relator talents. Schedule activities that allow you to get even closer to the people who keep you grounded and happy.

- ❏ Make an effort to socialize with your colleagues and team members outside of work. It can be as simple as lunch or coffee together. This will help you forge more connected relationships at work, which in turn can facilitate more effective teamwork and cooperation.

Working With Others Who Have Relator

- ❏ People with Relator enjoy developing genuine bonds with their colleagues. These relationships take time to build, so you must invest in them on a regular basis.

- ❏ Tell people with Relator directly that you care about them. More than likely, this language will not sound inappropriate, and they will welcome it. They organize their life around their close relationships, so they will want to know where they stand with you.

- ❏ Trust people who have Relator with confidential information. They are loyal, place a high value on trust and will not betray yours.

RESPONSIBILITY

Your Responsibility theme forces you to take psychological ownership for anything you commit to, and whether large or small, you feel emotionally bound to follow it through to completion. Your good name depends on it. If for some reason you cannot deliver, you automatically start to look for ways to make it up to the other person. Apologies are not enough. Excuses and rationalizations are totally unacceptable. You will not quite be able to live with yourself until you have made restitution. This conscientiousness, this near obsession for doing things right, and your impeccable ethics combine to create your reputation: utterly dependable. When assigning new responsibilities, people will look to you first because they know it will get done. When people come to you for help — and they soon will — you must be selective. Your willingness to volunteer may sometimes lead you to take on more than you should.

Responsibility Sounds Like This:

Kelly G., operations manager: "The country manager in Sweden called me in November and said, 'Kelly, could you please not ship my inventory until January 1.' I said, 'Sure. Sounds like a good plan.' I told my people about the plan and thought I had all the bases covered. On December 31, however, when I was checking my messages while on a ski slope, making sure everything was hunky-dory, I saw that his order had already been shipped and invoiced. I had to call immediately and tell him what happened. He's a nice man, so he didn't use any four-letter words, but he was very angry and very disappointed. I felt terrible. An apology wasn't enough. I needed to fix it. I called our controller from the chalet, and that afternoon we figured out a way to put the value of his inventory back on our books and clean it off his. It took most of the weekend, but it was the right thing to do."

Nigel T., sales executive: "I used to think that there was a piece of metal in my hand and a magnet on the ceiling. I would just volunteer for everything. I have had to learn how to manage that because not only would I end up with too much on my plate, but I would also wind up thinking that everything was my fault. I realize now that I can't be responsible for everything in the world — that's God's job."

Harry B., outplacement consultant: "I was just a young bank manager in one of the branches when the president of the company decided that he wanted to foreclose on a property. I said, 'That's fine, but we have a responsibility to give the people full value for their property.' He didn't see it that way. He wanted to sell the property to a friend of his for what was owed, and he said my problem was that I couldn't separate my business ethics from my personal ethics. I told him that was correct. I couldn't because I didn't believe — and still don't believe — that you can have two standards. So I quit the firm and went back to earning five dollars an hour working for the forestry service picking up trash. Since my wife and I were trying to support our two kids and make ends meet, it was a hard decision for me to make. But looking back, on one level, it really wasn't hard at all. I simply couldn't function in an organization with those kinds of ethics."

Ideas for Action

❑ Emphasize your sense of responsibility when job hunting. During interviews, describe your desire to be held fully accountable for the success or failure of projects, your intense dislike of unfinished work, and your need to "make it right" if a commitment is not met.

- ❏ Keep volunteering for more responsibility than your experience seems to warrant. You thrive on responsibility, and you can deal with it very effectively.

- ❏ Align yourself with others who share your sense of responsibility. You will flourish when working with people who share your determination to get things done.

- ❏ Tell your manager that you work best when given the freedom to follow through on your commitments — that you don't need to check in during a project, just at the end. You can be trusted to get it done.

- ❏ Push yourself to say no. Because you are instinctively responsible, it might sometimes be difficult to refuse opportunities. For this reason, you must be selective. Ask for more responsibility in only the areas that matter most to you.

- ❏ You naturally take ownership of every project you are involved in. Make sure that your capacity to own does not keep you from sharing responsibility. Allow others the opportunity to experience the challenges of ownership. In doing so, you will contribute to their growth and development.

- ❏ Learn to manage your Responsibility talents by considering whether you really are the person who should be handling a particular issue. Defer to your existing responsibilities and goals before undertaking additional burdens, as you may end up skimping on quality if you have too many tasks or competing demands.

- Partner with someone especially talented in Discipline or Focus. This person can help you stay on track and prevent you from becoming overloaded.

- Working with a like-minded, responsible colleague is satisfying for you. Be sure to clarify expectations and boundaries so that each person can feel ownership for their particular tasks — without stepping on each other's toes.

- Responsible individuals like to know they have "delivered" on their commitments, so create metrics and goals to gauge how effectively you meet your obligations. Also, make sure you have explicit and concrete expectations so that there is no question regarding quality outcomes and so that you can hit the mark as promised.

Working With Others Who Have Responsibility

- People with Responsibility define themselves by their ability to live up to their commitments. It will be intensely frustrating for them to work with people who don't.

- People with Responsibility dislike sacrificing quality for speed, so be careful not to rush them. In discussing their work, talk about its quality first.

- Help people with Responsibility avoid taking on too much, particularly if they are lacking in Discipline talents. Help them see that one more burden may result in their dropping the ball — a notion they will loathe.

RESTORATIVE

You love to solve problems. Whereas some are dismayed when they encounter yet another breakdown, you can be energized by it. You enjoy the challenge of analyzing the symptoms, identifying what is wrong and finding the solution. You may prefer practical problems or conceptual ones or personal ones. You may seek out specific kinds of problems that you have met many times before and that you are confident you can fix. Or you may feel the greatest push when faced with complex and unfamiliar problems. Your exact preferences are determined by your other themes and experiences. But what is certain is that you enjoy bringing things back to life. It is a wonderful feeling to identify the undermining factor(s), eradicate them and restore something to its true glory. Intuitively, you know that without your intervention, this thing — this machine, this technique, this person, this company — might have ceased to function. You fixed it, resuscitated it, rekindled its vitality. Phrasing it the way you might, you saved it.

Restorative Sounds Like This:

Nigel L., software designer: "I have these vivid memories of my childhood woodworking bench with hammers and nails and wood. I used to love fixing things and putting things together and making everything just so. And now with computer programs, it's the same thing. You write the program, and if it doesn't work, you have to go back and redo it and fix it until it works."

Jan K., internist: "This theme plays in my life in so many ways. For example, my first love was surgery. I love trauma, love being in the OR, love sewing. I just love fixing things in the

OR. Then again, some of my best moments have been sitting at the bedside of a dying patient, just talking together. It is incredibly rewarding to watch someone make the transition from anger to acceptance about grief, to tie up loose ends with family members and to pass with dignity. And then with my kids, this theme fires every day. When I see my three-year-old buttoning her sweater for the first time and she buttons it crooked, I feel this powerful urge to walk up and rebutton the sweater. I have to resist, of course, because she has to learn, but, boy, it's really hard."

Marie T., television producer: "Producing a morning TV program is a fundamentally clumsy process. If I didn't like solving problems, this job would drive me up the wall. Every day, something serious goes wrong, and I have to find the problem, fix it and move on to the next one. If I can do that well, I feel rejuvenated. On the other hand, if I go home and a problem remains unsolved, then I feel the opposite. I feel defeated."

Ideas for Action

- ❏ Seek roles in which you are paid to solve problems or in which your success depends on your ability to restore and resolve. You might particularly enjoy roles in medicine, consulting, computer programming or customer service.

- ❏ Don't be afraid to let others know that you enjoy fixing problems. It comes naturally to you, but many people shy away from problems. You can help.

- ❏ Give yourself a break. Your Restorative talents might lead you to be overly self-critical. Try to redirect this either toward things about yourself that can be fixed, such as knowledge or skill deficits, or toward external, tangible problems.

- ❏ Let other people solve their own problems. You might want to rush in and solve things for them, but by doing that, you might hinder their learning. Watch out for this, particularly if you are in a manager, coach, teacher or parent role.

- ❏ Turnaround situations activate your natural forte. Use your Restorative talents to devise a plan of attack to revitalize a flagging project, organization, business or team.

- ❏ Leverage your Restorative talents not only to tackle existing problems, but also to anticipate and prevent problems before they occur. Share your foresight and your solutions with others, and you will prove yourself a valuable partner.

- ❏ Study your chosen subject closely to become adept at identifying what causes certain problems to recur. This sort of expertise will lead you to the solution that much faster.

- ❏ Think about ways you can improve your skills and knowledge. Identify any gaps you have and the courses you can take to fill them.

- ❏ Constant improvement is one of your hallmarks. Seek opportunities to enhance your abilities through a demanding field, activity or endeavor that requires exceptional skill and/or knowledge.

Restorative

- Use your Restorative talents to think of ways to "problem proof" your work. Identify existing and potential issues, and design systems or processes to prevent errors in the future.

Working With Others Who Have Restorative

- Ask people with Restorative for their observations when you want to identify a problem within your organization. Their insights will be particularly acute.

- When a situation in your organization needs immediate improvement, turn to people with Restorative for help. They will not panic. Instead, they will respond in a focused, professional way.

- Offer your support when people with Restorative meet a particularly thorny problem. Because they define themselves by their ability to cope, they may well feel personally defeated if a problem remains unresolved. Help them through it.

SELF-ASSURANCE

Self-Assurance is similar to self-confidence. In the deepest part of you, you have faith in your strengths. You know that you are able — able to take risks, able to meet new challenges, able to stake claims and, most important, able to deliver. But Self-Assurance is more than just self-confidence. Blessed with the theme of Self-Assurance, you have confidence not only in your abilities but in your judgment. When you look at the world, you know that your perspective is unique and distinct. And because no one sees exactly what you see, you know that no one can make your decisions for you. No one can tell you what to think. They can guide. They can suggest. But you alone have the authority to form conclusions, make decisions and act. This authority, this final accountability for the living of your life, does not intimidate you. On the contrary, it feels natural to you. No matter what the situation, you seem to know what the right decision is. This theme lends you an aura of certainty. Unlike many, you are not easily swayed by someone else's arguments, no matter how persuasive they may be. This Self-Assurance may be quiet or loud, depending on your other themes, but it is solid. It is strong. Like the keel of a ship, it withstands many different pressures and keeps you on your course.

Self-Assurance Sounds Like This:

Pam D., public service executive: "I was raised on a remote farm in Idaho, and I attended a small rural school. One day, I returned home from school and announced to my mother that I was changing schools. Earlier in the day, my teacher had explained that our school had too many kids and that three kids would have to move to a different school. I thought about it for a moment, liked the idea of meeting new people and decided I would be one of them — even though it meant getting up half an hour earlier and traveling farther on the bus. I was five years old."

James K., salesman: "I never second-guess myself. Whether I am buying a birthday present or a house, when I make my decision, it feels to me as if I had no choice. There was only one decision to make, and I made it. It's easy for me to sleep at night. My gut is final, loud and very persuasive."

Deborah C., ER nurse: "If we have a death in the ER, people call on me to deal with the family because of my confidence. Just yesterday, we had a problem with a young psychotic girl who was screaming that the devil was inside her. The other nurses were afraid, but I knew what to do. I went in and said, 'Kate, come on, lie back. Let's say the Baruch. It's a Jewish prayer. It goes like this: Baruch Atah Adonai, Eloheinu Melech Haolam.' She responded, 'Say it slowly so that I can say it back to you.' I did, and then she said it back to me slowly. She wasn't Jewish, but this calm came over her. She dropped back against her pillow and said, 'Thank you. That's all I needed.'"

Ideas for Action

- ❑ Look for start-up situations for which no rulebook exists. You will be at your best when you are asked to make many decisions.

- ❑ Seek roles in which you convince people to see your point of view. Your Self-Assurance talents (especially when combined with Command or Activator talents) can be extremely persuasive. Leadership, sales, legal or entrepreneurial roles might suit you.

❏ Let your self-confidence show. It can be contagious and will help the people around you grow.

❏ Realize that sometimes you will find it hard to put your certainty or intuition into words, possibly leading others to see you as self-righteous. Explain that your confidence does not mean that they should withhold their opinions. It might not seem like it to them, but you do want to hear their ideas. Your conviction doesn't mean that you are unwilling to listen to them.

❏ Your independent streak can leave you standing alone. If this happens, make sure you are out in front, or partner with someone who can help others see how they can benefit from following you.

❏ Partner with someone with strong Strategic, Deliberative or Futuristic talents. This person can help you assess the goals to which you commit. You need this help because once you set your sights on a goal, you are likely to stay with it until you achieve it.

❏ Your exceptionally hard work and long hours are natural products of the passion and confidence you feel about your work. Don't assume that others are similarly wired.

❏ You can be decisive, even when things get dynamic and distracting. When there is chaos around you, intentionally display and share the calm and certainty within you. This will give others comfort and security.

Self-Assurance

- Set ambitious goals. Don't hesitate to reach for what others see as impractical and impossible, but what you see as merely bold and exciting — and most importantly — achievable with some heroics and a little luck. Your Self-Assurance talents can lead to achievements that you may not have otherwise even imagined.

- You don't have a great need for direction and support from others. This could make you particularly effective in situations that require independent thinking and action. Recognize and actively contribute the value of your Self-Assurance talents when confidence and self-control are crucial.

Working With Others Who Have Self-Assurance

- If you are working on a team with people who have Self-Assurance, give them leeway in making decisions. They will neither want nor require hand-holding.

- Help people with Self-Assurance understand that their decisions and actions do produce outcomes. They are most effective when they believe they are in control of their world. Highlight practices that work.

- Although the self-confidence that people with Self-Assurance have can often prove useful, if they overclaim or make some major misjudgments, be sure to point it out immediately. They need clear feedback to inform their instincts.

SIGNIFICANCE

You want to be very significant in the eyes of other people. In the truest sense of the word you want to be recognized. You want to be heard. You want to stand out. You want to be known. In particular, you want to be known and appreciated for the unique strengths you bring. You feel a need to be admired as credible, professional and successful. Likewise, you want to associate with others who are credible, professional and successful. And if they aren't, you will push them to achieve until they are. Or you will move on. An independent spirit, you want your work to be a way of life rather than a job, and in that work you want to be given free rein, the leeway to do things your way. Your yearnings feel intense to you, and you honor those yearnings. And so your life is filled with goals, achievements or qualifications that you crave. Whatever your focus — and each person is distinct — your Significance theme will keep pulling you upward, away from the mediocre toward the exceptional. It is the theme that keeps you reaching.

Significance Sounds Like This:

Mary P., healthcare executive: "Women are told almost from day one, 'Don't be too proud. Don't stand tall.' That kind of thing. But I've learned that it's okay to have power, it's okay to have pride and it's okay to have a big ego — and also that I need to manage it and drive it in the right directions."

Kathie J., partner in a law firm: "Ever since I can remember, I have had the feeling that I was special, that I could take charge and make things happen. Back in the '60s, I was the first woman partner in my firm, and I can still recall walking into boardroom after boardroom and being the only woman. It's strange, thinking back. It was tough, but I actually think I enjoyed the pressure of standing out. I enjoyed being the 'woman' partner. Why? Because I knew that I would be very hard to forget. I knew everyone would notice me and pay attention to me."

John L., physician: "All through my life, I felt that I was on stage. I am always aware of an audience. If I am sitting with a patient, I want the patient to see me as the best doctor they have ever had. If I am teaching medical students, I want to stand out as the best medical educator they have ever had. I want to win the Educator of the Year award. My boss is a big audience for me. Disappointing her would kill me. It's scary to think that part of my self-esteem is in other people's hands, but then again, it keeps me on my toes."

Ideas for Action

❏ Choose jobs or positions in which you can determine your own tasks and actions. You will enjoy the exposure that comes with independence.

❏ Your reputation is important to you, so decide what it should be and tend to it in the smallest detail. For example, identify and earn a designation that will add to your credibility, write an article that will give you visibility, or volunteer to speak in front of a group that will admire your achievements.

❏ Share your dreams and goals with your family or closest friends and colleagues. Their expectations will keep you reaching.

- Stay focused on performance. Your Significance talents will drive you to claim outstanding goals. Your performance had better match those goals, or others might label you as a big talker.

- You will perform best when your performance is visible. Look for opportunities that put you on center stage. Stay away from roles that hide you behind the scenes.

- Leading crucial teams or significant projects brings out your best. Your greatest motivation may come when the stakes are at their highest. Let others know that when the game is on the line, you want the ball.

- Make a list of the goals, achievements and qualifications you crave, and post them where you will see them every day. Use this list to inspire yourself.

- Identify your best moment of recognition or praise. What was it for? Who gave it to you? Who was the audience? What do you have to do to recreate that moment?

- Unless you also possess dominant Self-Assurance talents, accept that you might fear failure. Don't let this fear prevent you from staking claims to excellence. Instead, use it to focus on ensuring that your performance matches your claims.

- You might have a natural awareness of what other people think of you. You may have a specific audience that you want to like you, and you will do whatever it takes to win their approval and applause. Be aware that while reliance on the approval of others could be problematic, there is nothing wrong with wanting to be liked or admired by the key people in your life.

Working With Others Who Have Significance

- ❑ When working with people who have Significance, be aware of their need for independence. If you do need to challenge them, understand that a confrontation may ensue.

- ❑ Acknowledge that people with Significance thrive on meaningful recognition for their contributions. Give them room to maneuver, but never ignore them.

- ❑ Give people with Significance the opportunity to stand out, to be known. They enjoy the pressure of being the focal point of attention.

STRATEGIC

The Strategic theme enables you to sort through the clutter and find the best route. It is not a skill that can be taught. It is a distinct way of thinking, a special perspective on the world at large. This perspective allows you to see patterns where others simply see complexity. Mindful of these patterns, you play out alternative scenarios, always asking, "What if this happened? Okay, well what if this happened?" This recurring question helps you see around the next corner. There you can evaluate accurately the potential obstacles. Guided by where you see each path leading, you start to make selections. You discard the paths that lead nowhere. You discard the paths that lead straight into resistance. You discard the paths that lead into a fog of confusion. You cull and make selections until you arrive at the chosen path — your strategy. Armed with your strategy, you strike forward. This is your Strategic theme at work: "What if?" Select. Strike.

Strategic Sounds Like This:

Liam C., manufacturing plant manager: "It seems as if I can always see the consequences before anyone else can. I have to say to people, 'Lift up your eyes; look down the road a ways. Let's talk about where we are going to be next year so that when we get to this time next year, we don't have the same problems.' It seems obvious to me, but some people are just too focused on this month's numbers, and everything is driven by that."

Vivian T., television producer: "I used to love logic problems when I was a kid — you know, the ones where 'if A implies B, and B equals C, does A equal C?' Still today, I am always playing out repercussions, seeing where things lead. I think it makes me a great interviewer. I know that nothing is an accident; every sign, every word, every tone of voice has significance. So I watch for these clues and play them out in my head, see where they lead and then plan my questions to take advantage of what I have seen in my head."

Simon T., human resources executive: "We really needed to take the union on at some stage, and I saw an opportunity — a very good issue to take them on. I could see that they were going in a direction that would lead them into all kinds of trouble if they continued following it. Lo and behold, they did continue following it, and when they arrived, there I was, ready and waiting. I suppose it just comes naturally to me to predict what someone else is going to do. And then when that person reacts, I can respond immediately because I have sat down and said, 'Okay, if they do this, we'll do this. If they do that, then we'll do this other thing.' It's like when you tack in a sailboat. You head in one direction, but you jinx one way, then another, planning and reacting, planning and reacting."

Ideas for Action

❏ Take the time to fully reflect or muse about a goal that you want to achieve until the related patterns and issues emerge for you. Remember that this musing time is essential to strategic thinking.

❏ You can see repercussions more clearly than others can. Take advantage of this ability by planning your range of responses in detail. There is little point in knowing where events will lead if you are not ready when you get there.

- ❑ Find a group that you think does important work, and contribute your strategic thinking. You can be a leader with your ideas.

- ❑ Your strategic thinking will be necessary to keep a vivid vision from deteriorating into an ordinary pipe dream. Fully consider all possible paths toward making the vision a reality. Wise forethought can remove obstacles before they appear.

- ❑ Make yourself known as a resource for consultation with those who are stumped by a particular problem or hindered by a particular obstacle or barrier. By naturally seeing a way when others are convinced there is no way, you will lead them to success.

- ❑ You are likely to anticipate potential issues more easily than others. Though your awareness of possible danger might be viewed as negativity by some, you must share your insights if you are going to avoid these pitfalls. To prevent misperception of your intent, point out not only the future obstacle, but also a way to prevent or overcome it. Trust your insights, and use them to ensure the success of your efforts.

- ❑ Help others understand that your strategic thinking is not an attempt to belittle their ideas, but is instead a natural propensity to consider all the facets of a plan objectively. Rather than being a naysayer, you are actually trying to examine ways to ensure that the goal is accomplished, come what may. Your talents will allow you to consider others' perspectives while keeping your end goal in sight.

Strategic

- ❏ Trust your intuitive insights as often as possible. Even though you might not be able to explain them rationally, your intuitions are created by a brain that instinctively anticipates and projects. Have confidence in these perceptions.

- ❏ Partner with someone with strong Activator talents. With this person's need for action and your need for anticipation, you can forge a powerful partnership.

- ❏ Make sure that you are involved in the front end of new initiatives or enterprises. Your innovative yet procedural approach will be critical to the genesis of a new venture because it will keep its creators from developing deadly tunnel vision.

Working With Others Who Have Strategic

- ❏ Involve people who have Strategic in planning sessions. Ask them, "If this happened, what should we expect? If that happened, what should we expect?"

- ❏ Always give people with Strategic ample time to think through a situation before asking for their input. They aren't likely to voice their opinion until they have played out a couple of scenarios in their mind.

- ❏ When you hear or read about strategies that worked in your field, share them with people who have Strategic. It will stimulate their thinking.

WOO

Woo stands for winning others over. You enjoy the challenge of meeting new people and getting them to like you. Strangers are rarely intimidating to you. On the contrary, strangers can be energizing. You are drawn to them. You want to learn their names, ask them questions and find some area of common interest so that you can strike up a conversation and build rapport. Some people shy away from starting up conversations because they worry about running out of things to say. You don't. Not only are you rarely at a loss for words; you actually enjoy initiating with strangers because you derive satisfaction from breaking the ice and making a connection. Once that connection is made, you are quite happy to wrap it up and move on. There are new people to meet, new rooms to work, new crowds to mingle in. In your world there are no strangers, only friends you haven't met yet — lots of them.

Woo Sounds Like This:

Deborah C., publishing executive: "I have made best friends out of people that I have met passing in the doorway. I mean, it's awful, but wooing is part of who I am. All my taxi drivers propose to me."

Marilyn K., college president: "I don't believe I'm looking for friends, but people call me a friend. I call people and say, 'I love you,' and I mean it because I love people easily. But friends? I don't have many friends. I don't think I am looking for friends. I am looking for connections. And I am really good at that because I know how to achieve common ground with people."

Anna G., nurse: "I think I am a little shy sometimes. Usually I won't make the first step out. But I do know how to put people at ease. A lot of my job is just humor. If the patient is not very receptive, my role becomes that of a stand-up comedian. I'll say to an eighty-year-old patient, 'Hi, you handsome guy. Sit up. Let me get your shirt off. That's good. Take your shirt off. Whoa, what a chest on this man!' With kids, you have to start very slowly and say something like, 'How old are you?' If they say, 'Ten,' then I say, 'Really? When I was your age, I was eleven'— silly stuff like that to break the ice."

Ideas for Action

❏ Choose a job in which you can interact with many people over the course of a day.

❏ Deliberately build the network of people who know you. Tend to it by checking in with each person at least once a month.

❏ Join local organizations, volunteer for committees and find out how to get on the social lists of the influential people where you live.

❏ Learn the names of as many people as you can. Create a file of the people you know, and add names as you become acquainted. Include a snippet of personal information — such as their birthday, favorite color, hobby or favorite sports team.

❏ In social situations, take responsibility for helping put reserved people at ease.

- Find the right words to explain that networking is part of your style. If you don't claim this theme, others might mistake it for insincerity and wonder why you are being so friendly.

- Partner with someone with dominant Relator or Empathy talents. This person can solidify the relationships that you begin.

- Your Woo talents give you the ability to quicken the pulse of your surroundings. Recognize the power of your presence and how you open doors for an exchange of ideas. By simply starting conversations that engage others and bring talented people together, you will take performance up a notch — or several.

- The first moments of any social occasion are crucial to how comfortable people will be and how they will remember the event. Whenever possible, be one of the first people others meet. Your capacity for meeting and greeting new people will help to quickly put them at ease.

- Practice ways to charm and engage others. For example, research people before you meet them so you can talk about your common interests.

Working With Others Who Have Woo

- Help people who have Woo meet new people every day. They can put strangers at ease and help them feel comfortable with your organization.

- ❏ If you need to extend your own network, reach out to people with strong Woo talents. They will help you broaden your own connections and get what you want.

- ❏ Understand that people with Woo value having a wide network of friends. If they are quick to meet and greet and then move on, do not take it personally.

VFAQ
(**Very** Frequently Asked Question)

If I have already taken the original CliftonStrengths assessment, should I take the updated version?

It's up to you. While we have fine-tuned the assessment to be slightly faster and more precise, the language of 34 themes remains the same. So if you have taken the original CliftonStrengths assessment, your results remain as valid now as they were when you completed the assessment.

The primary difference between the original version and the updated version is not in the assessment itself, but in the results and resources available. Because the strengths development guide includes customized Strengths Insights, which are based on more than 5,000 unique combinations of responses within the updated assessment, we are only able to produce this comprehensive guide if you take the updated version.

If you have taken the original version and you decide to take the updated version, you may find that a few of your top five themes are different than they were the first time. Given the basic odds and statistics of calculating a ranking of 34 dimensions, even if you take the same version of CliftonStrengths again a few months later, it is not unusual for a couple of your top five themes to change. With more than 33 million unique combinations of top five themes, the CliftonStrengths assessment is very different from basic personality tests that classify you, for example, as *either* an extrovert *or* an introvert.

Based on our calculations, if you compare your results from the original version of the assessment to your results from the updated version, there's a strong chance that at least three of your top five themes will remain the same. And in most cases, at least four themes will appear in your top five both times. Perhaps the most important thing to understand for your development is that if you do see a new theme in your top five, it was likely in your top 10 before. So you have not "lost" a theme, but instead now have the opportunity to see a theme or two that had been hiding just below the radar.

Gallup Press exists to educate and inform the people who govern, manage, teach and lead the world's 7 billion citizens. Each book meets Gallup's requirements of integrity, trust and independence and is based on Gallup-approved science and research.

This packet contains:

YOUR UNIQUE ACCESS CODE* TO TAKE THE CLIFTONSTRENGTHS® ASSESSMENT.

* This access code is valid for one use only. Do not buy this book if this packet has been opened.

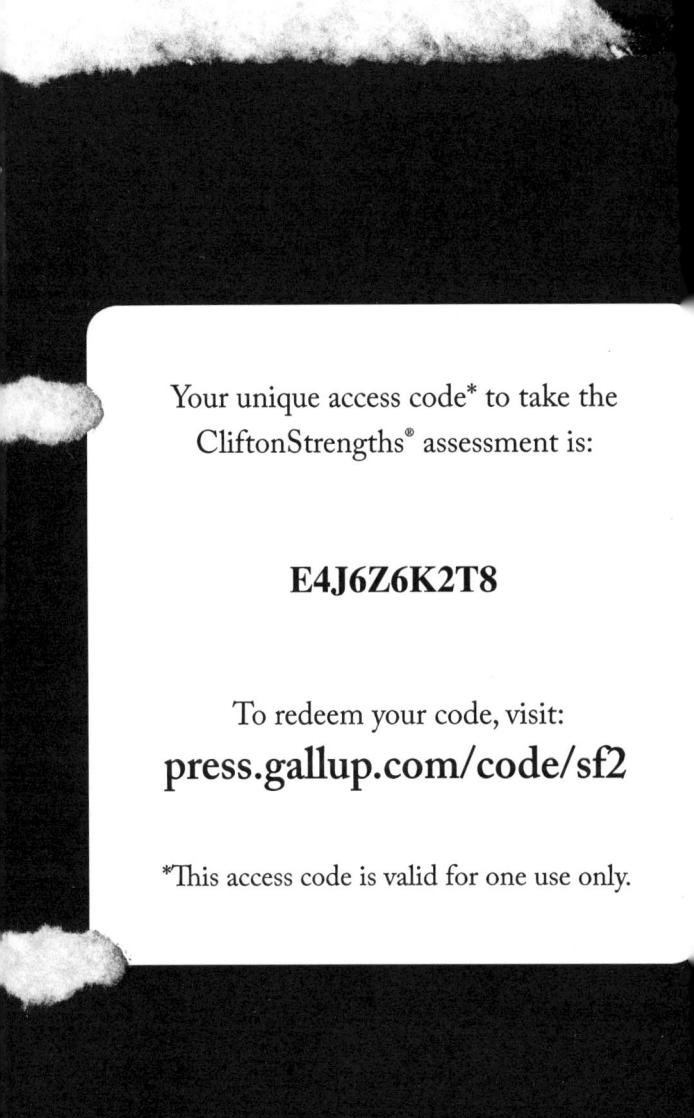

Your unique access code* to take the CliftonStrengths® assessment is:

E4J6Z6K2T8

To redeem your code, visit:
press.gallup.com/code/sf2

*This access code is valid for one use only.

This packet contains:

YOUR UNIQUE ACCESS CODE* TO TAKE THE CLIFTONSTRENGTHS® ASSESSMENT.

* This access code is valid for one use only. Do not buy this book if this packet has been opened.